Flower Projects

For the Home

Flower Projects

For the Home

Joanna Sheen

MEREHURST

Published in 1994 by Merehurst Limited
Ferry House, 51-57 Lacy Road, Putney, London SW15 1PR
Text © copyright Joanna Sheen 1994
Photographs © copyright Merehurst Limited 1994

ISBN 1-85391-381-2

A catalogue record for this book is available from the British Library.

Managing Editor **Heather Dewhurst**
Edited by **Diana Lodge**
Designed by **Lisa Tai**
Photography by **Debbie Patterson**; with the exception of pages 92-3, 96-9,
100-101, 104-7, 110-11, 114-17, 120-23, 126-31, 136-9, 142-3, 146-7, 150-51,
154-5, 158-61, 164-7 and 170-75, which were photographed by **Mike Evans**.
Styling Assistant **Camilla Bambrough**

Acknowledgements
Merehurst would like to thank the following for loaning props for photography: The Dining Room
Shop, 62-64 White Hart Lane, London SW13; Georgina Von Etzdorf, 149 Sloane Street, London
SW1; Modus Vicendi, Stand GO, 80 Ground Floor, Alfies Antique Market, Church Street, London
NW1; Paperchase, 213 Tottenham Court Road, London W1; Tobias & the Angel, 68 White Hart
Lane, London SW13; Basia Zarzycka, Front Shop, Antiquarius, 135 Kings Road, London SW3.

Typesetting by **Litho Link Limited**
Colour separation by **Fotographics Ltd UK – Hong Kong**
Printed in Italy by **New Interlitho S.p.A.**

*Merehurst is a leading publisher of craft books and has an excellent range of titles
to suit all levels. Please send to the address above for our free catalogue, stating
the title of this book.*

Contents

Introduction 6

CHAPTER 1 – Arrangements with Fresh Flowers 8
Daisy garland 10 • A fireplace arrangement 14
Marble display 18 • Anemones in terracotta 22
Rustic basket 24 • Table center 28
Tied bunch 32 • A circular arrangement 36
A basket for a bedroom 40 • Rose tree & Garden posy 42
Fruits and flowers 48 • Conditioning flowers and foliage 52

CHAPTER 2 – Using Scented Flowers 54
Lavender and roses 56 • Rose pot pourri & Herbal wreath 60
Chilli kitchen wreath 66 • Fruity pot pourri & Perfumed straw hat 70
Bath oil, cologne & Lavender-scented pomander 76
Fragrant flowers in terracotta 82 • Scented flower basics 86

CHAPTER 3 – Designs with Dried Flowers 88
A basket of garden flowers 90 • Dolly wreath 94
A kitchen wall basket 98 • Golden wedding ring & Table centerpiece 102
Family room arrangement 108 • Pot pourri basket & Topiary tree 112
Celebration tree and Flowery picnic basket 118
Hall mirror & Christmas arrangement 124 • Drying flowers 130

CHAPTER 4 – Pressed Flower Projects 132
Greetings card and gift tag 134 • Family album 140
Wedding photograph album 144
The four seasons – *Spring* 148 – *Summer* 152 – *Fall & Winter* 156
Decorated calligraphy 162 • Terracotta bowl & Garden posy 168
Pressing flowers 174

$\mathcal{I}$ntroduction

Flowers, in any shape or form, can be one of the most uplifting sights. A host of golden daffodils or a single snowdrop, a beautiful display of dried roses or a tiny posy of garden flowers picked by a child – all of these bring instant pleasure.

In this book is a wide range of projects, showing how flowers can be displayed when fresh or dried, how the petals can be used for pot pourri, and how their scents can be enjoyed to the full.

The first chapter contains ideas for fresh flower arrangements, ranging from a simple tied bunch of flowers to a lovely topiary tree made with fresh roses. The second chapter examines ways of capturing and exploiting the delicate scents of flowers and herbs, and contains a range of pot pourri mixtures, scented wreaths, and bath oils. Dried flower arrangements are the subject of the third chapter, which contains a range of enchanting and unusual designs for your home. The final chapter takes up the Victorian pastime of flower pressing, with a selection of attractive flower pictures made with pressed flowers. I hope that you will enjoy the ideas suggested in this book, and go on to create new designs of your own.

Chapter 1

*A*rrangements with Fresh Flowers

Flowers are one of Nature's greatest creations and the enjoyment and beauty they can bring is immense. There is absolutely no need to have any talent for flower arranging, just the gift of enjoying beautiful things. Flowers can be as inspiring placed in a clean jelly jar as worked on for hours in a complicated arrangement. The most important thing is to treat the flowers correctly, which includes keeping their water filled up so that they can last as long as possible. If you want to go further than admiring flowers in a jelly jar, then arranging flowers with complementary foliage, and other colors and textures can be a very exciting pastime. There is no limit to the time you can spend arranging flowers; you can achieve simple ideas in minutes, or pass an enjoyable morning creating a masterpiece – the choice is yours! This book includes a range of projects, from simple floating flowers, to more advanced ideas for filling a fireplace or decorating a Christmas topiary tree.

Daisy garland

*Garlands of flowers decorating an entrance or gate can make
a stunning focal point. Although they look complicated and
expensive, they are neither; with some patience and a reasonable
collection of material, they can be made in a few hours and will
gather an enormous number of compliments!*

$\mathcal{D}$aisy garland

Many different ingredients are suitable for inclusion in a garland. You will need several types of foliage, as these act as useful padding, and some fairly solid flowers – dainty ones can be missed among the collection of ingredients. Roses always look lovely, but they are an expensive choice, as you would need about two dozen at least for a garland of this size. Using daisy sprays, however, as I have here, you can produce a lovely effect for a modest cost. You will need a large bunch of both pink and white daisies (enough to produce about 36 heads of each), a bunch of eucalyptus, senecio and some conifer, rosemary and a small bunch of gypsophila. This would be enough to produce a garland approximately 3ft in length.

INGREDIENTS

Flowers and foliage,
as above

ع

4ft of bathrobe cord

ع

6ft of ribbon, 1½–2in wide

ع

One reel of very fine wire

ع

1 Form each of the ingredients into about 12 small bunches, some 2–3in long. The daisies should have three heads per bunch, and the other bunches should be roughly the same size. Make a loop at each end of the cord and bind with wire; bind on the first few bunches of foliage, making sure you have a well-balanced effect.

2 It is easier to use pieces of wire approximately 12in long rather than one long continuous piece, which might get knotted and tangled around the garland. Continue to bind on the bunches randomly, but always taking care that they are evenly distributed. Keep the bunches on top of the cord; do not allow it to slide so that you are binding bunches all around the cord, as you would require much more material to make a garland with flowers or foliage all around. If the garland will be viewed from the front and back, double the quantities.

3 Once you have covered a quarter of the cord, start again from the opposite end and work towards the middle. Continue adding bunches and binding firmly, keeping the stems on top of the cord. As you approach the middle (you can mark this with a small twist of wire), shorten the length of the stems and place them almost at right angles to the cord. Lay the finished garland out and check that there are no bald patches and the width is even. Make two loops and tails from the ribbon (see page 48) and wire them into each end at the base of the cord loops.

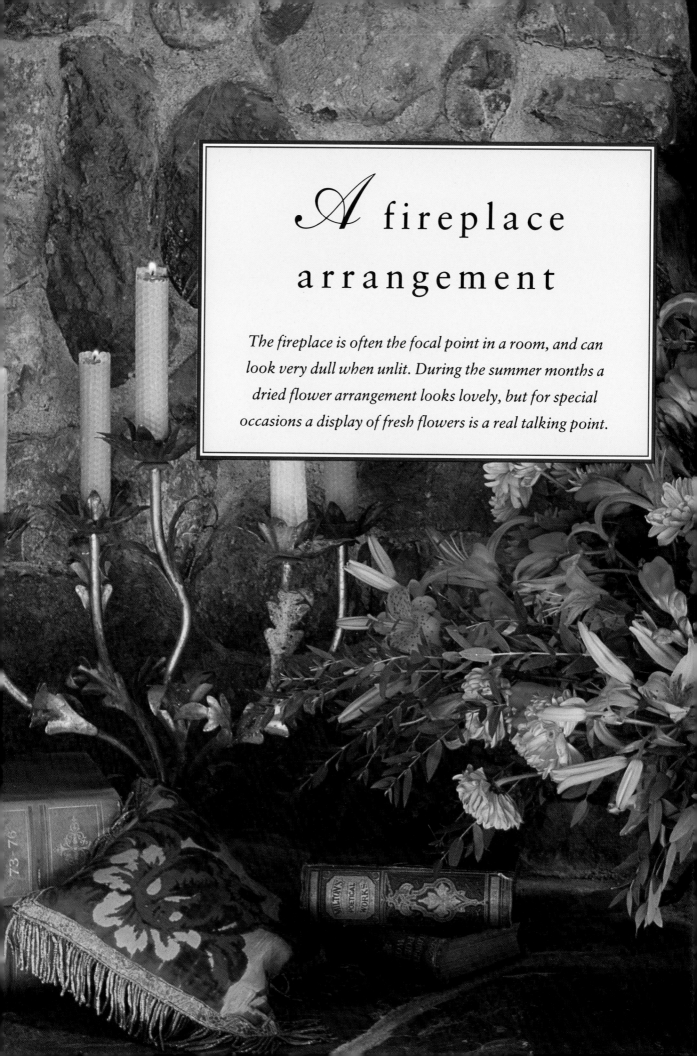

A fireplace arrangement

The fireplace is often the focal point in a room, and can look very dull when unlit. During the summer months a dried flower arrangement looks lovely, but for special occasions a display of fresh flowers is a real talking point.

73-76

$\mathcal{A}$ fireplace arrangement

If you have access to flowers from your garden, even a large arrangement such as this can cost very little to put together. The copper container can double as a decorative log container when it is not in use as a vase! Foliage is very important to help fill an arrangement like this one; a design made with flowers on their own would use many more blooms than I have included here. If you enjoy having fresh flowers in the house, a good selection of foliage plants and shrubs in the garden are invaluable. This arrangement uses three bunches of eucalyptus, four bunches of red freesias, five stems of apricot-colored single chrysanthemums, and five stems of orange lilies.

INGREDIENTS

*Flowers and foliage,
see above*

*A large copper container,
12in in diameter*

*Five blocks of green
florist's foam*

1 Place the foam in the container – lining it first if there are any holes in the metal, and cutting the blocks if necessary. Add water, allowing it to soak into the foam. Insert the eucalyptus, making a fan with the highest point in the middle and the longest points at each side.

2 Cut a stem of chrysanthemum to the correct length – it should come just below the height of the longest piece of eucalyptus at the back. Clean away all the leaves that would go into the foam. Do likewise with the other pieces of chrysanthemum at the sides and front.

3 *The orange lilies go into the arrangement next; again, trim off any excess leaves at the base of each stem and cut it to the correct length by holding it roughly in position and allowing about 1–2in to go into the foam. Place all the lily stems into the arrangement.*

4 *Finally, insert the freesias. You will not need to trim the stems very much. They should be put in the main body of the arrangement to add a darker color. If you are unable to get these particular flowers, you could use either yellow freesias or golden chrysanthemums as a substitute.*

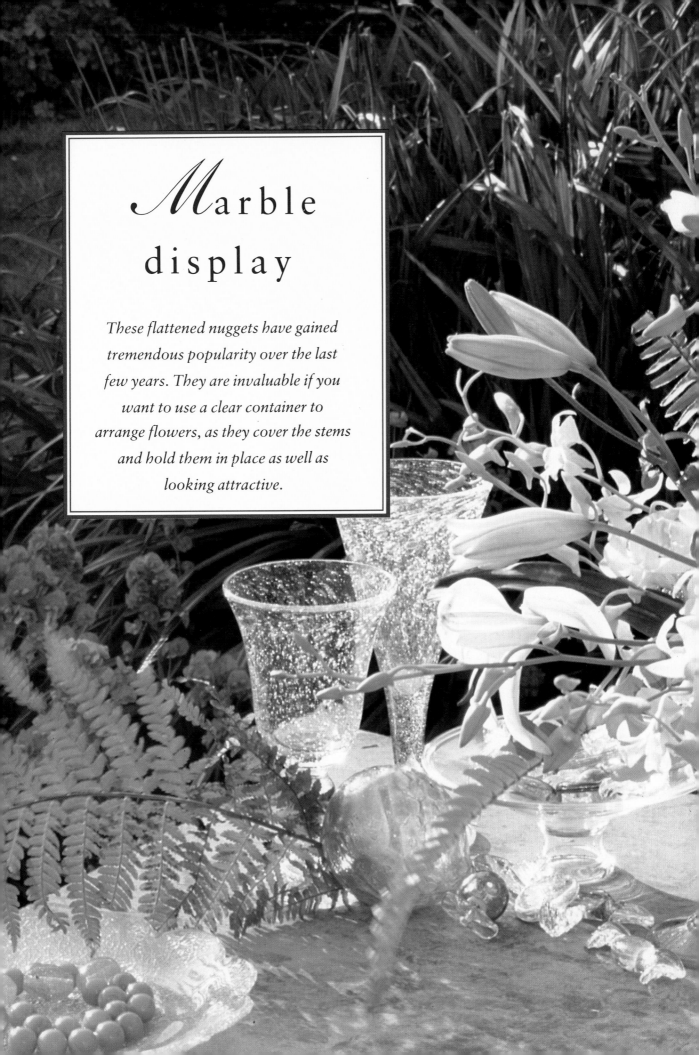

Marble display

These flattened nuggets have gained tremendous popularity over the last few years. They are invaluable if you want to use a clear container to arrange flowers, as they cover the stems and hold them in place as well as looking attractive.

$\mathcal{M}$arble display

Simple arrangements are often the prettiest and time is precious to us all. An arrangement like this can be made in a very short time and appreciated for at least a week. Using marbles or nuggets as a flower arranging aid is a relatively new idea and is now becoming very popular. They overcome the problem of unsightly stalks being visible when you use a clear glass container and they hold the stems in position, making arranging much easier (for suppliers, see page 48). Any flowers could be used in an arrangement like this, but the lilies and Singapore orchids used here last well. I have used three bunches (three stems in a bunch) of Singapore orchids and three stems of white lilies.

INGREDIENTS

Flowers and foliage,
see above

❧

Glass vase or jug

❧

Two jars of glass nuggets
(the exact quantity depends
upon the size of the vase)

1 Fill the container about two-thirds full with nuggets and add water until the level is just above the nuggets. The foliage used here are the ferns and leaves that come with the bunch of Singapore orchids. I used six pieces, pushing them into the nuggets and splaying them in a fan.

2 *Put the three stems of white lilies in position, forming a rough triangle. Make sure that you have taken off any leaves that would go below the surface of the water, as these would make the water smell after a short while.*

3 *Add the white Singapore orchids, one stem at a time. Make sure that the stems are held by the nuggets and place them all around the lilies. These orchids are not as expensive as they sound; the small bunches of three stems are readily available now, and are reasonably priced.*

*A*nemones in terracotta

Terracotta is usually regarded as suitable for outdoor use, but it can look stunning when used for informal arrangements indoors. Either waterproof the container by coating the inside with waterproof adhesive and blocking the hole in the base or, much more simply, put your flowers in a jelly jar hidden inside the container. Garden flowers are ideal for this type of arrangement, but something simple from a florist could also be attractive.

INGREDIENTS

12–15 Helleborus foetidus leaves

ༀ

3–4 bunches of mixed anemones

ༀ

One jelly jar (or seal the container, see above)

ༀ

One terracotta pot

1 Clean the pot if it has been outside, but do not scrub too hard as the discoloration is most attractive. Place the jelly jar inside the pot (or waterproof as mentioned above) and fill with water. Place the leaves around the pot in a random way to form a base for the flowers.

2 Place flowers in the container one at a time, mixing the colors randomly. Ensure that the stems are well down into the jar so that they can take up plenty of water. This is an informal arrangement, and the look should be natural – the backs of flowers and curves of stems can be as attractive as the full face.

Rustic basket

This rough country basket looks wonderful when casually filled with a collection of spring flowers. Rustic baskets and containers add so much to an informal arrangement of this type, and baskets are usually fairly easily available. Once you have built up a collection, they can be used over and over again!

$\mathcal{R}$ustic basket

Spring flowers are always beautiful, whether they are artistically arranged or just a bunch of daffodils abandoned in a jelly jar. The strong colors of the yellow miniature daffodils in this arrangement would brighten any corner of the house. The foliage is taken from the garden – trailing ivy, *Helleborus foetidus* foliage and flowers, and some pussy willow. This choice, however, is easily interchangeable with whatever foliage is readily available to you, whether it be garden bits and pieces or ferns and eucalyptus from a florist. The blue grape hyacinths make a lovely contrast against the yellow and green, but again another small spring flower could be used instead.

INGREDIENTS

*10–12 Helleborus foetidus
leaves and flowers, small
bunch of pussy willow, 7
pieces of trailing ivy and 5
of spurge (euphorbia), 9
miniature daffodils, 9 blue
grape hyacinths, and a few
strands of bear grass*

ঌ

*Half block of green
florist's foam*

ঌ

*Rustic basket, 8in
in diameter*

1 Soak the foam until it has taken up as much water as possible. Line the basket very carefully with plastic (this one came with a plastic lining), and then wedge the foam in the basket. Cover the foam with the hellebore leaves, set at various angles.

2 Add the other foliage ingredients. First, put the pussy willow at the back of the arrangement and at the front; then some trailing pieces of ivy; some spurge goes in the centre at the back, and some nearer the front. The hellebore flowers are then added to the centre of the arrangement.

3 Finally, add the remaining flowers in groups, varying the lengths of the stems so that they do not look too regimented. You could use more or less of any of these ingredients, depending upon availability. As a finishing touch, add some wispy strands of bear grass or other fine grass to lend a delicate feel to the edges of the arrangement.

Table center

Beeswax candles burn with a sweet smell and, together with the rosemary, add a lovely gentle fragrance to set the mood at a dinner party. Take care to keep the height of the arrangement fairly low or you will block everyone's view.

Table center

The center of the table can also be the center of attraction at a dinner party if you can find a few moments earlier in the day to prepare a small flower arrangement. Candles are always successful, and remember to include plenty of foliage as it makes a lovely background to the flowers. Given the choice I would leave out the flowers rather than the foliage! You will need a bunch of rosemary, a bunch of pink Peruvian lilies (*Alstroemeria*), 12–15 medium-to-large ivy leaves, about six sprigs of ivy (preferably with berries), and nine pink roses.

INGREDIENTS

*Flowers and foliage,
see above*

☙

*Three candleholders
and candles*

☙

*A half block of green
florist's foam*

☙

One shallow basket

1 Line the basket with plastic and soak the foam. Place the foam in the basket and push the pointed green candle holders into the foam. Cover the foam completely with ivy leaves, and have sprigs of ivy coming out of each end of the arrangement.

2 Add more ivy berries, if you have them, and some of the rosemary. The alstroemeria can be cut fairly short and placed in the arrangement one flower at a time rather than as a spray. If you cannot obtain rosemary, then use any other sweetly-scented herbal foliage, such as mint, sage, thyme or lavender. Make sure all foliage is well conditioned before you use it so that it doesn't droop before the party.

3 Lighten the arrangement with some sprigs of rosemary and then add the roses, placing them fairly low, where they will be seen. Check that the

arrangement looks pretty from all angles, as your guests are going to be sitting down and looking across at it from all sides. If you make the

arrangement standing up, you may find, when you join your guests at dinner and look across the table, that you have left a large gap in the flowers!

Tied bunch

There are several occasions for which you
might want to make an informal bouquet – as
a presentation after a speech, for example,
for a wedding or other celebration, or
simply as a thank-you present. Once you
have mastered the technique of binding the
flowers firmly, this style of bouquet is
simple to produce yourself.

$\mathcal{T}$ied bunch

Many people prefer to use a minimal amount of foliage in bouquets and arrangements, but I think the foliage is just as important as the flowers and provides the green, gray or rich fall colors that act as a foil for the tones of the flowers. This bunch uses flowering privet and shrubby honeysuckle (*Lonicera purpusii*), the latter having leaves of a clear lime green which works well with the intense pink roses and the strong blue iris. The flowering currant (*Ribes sanguineum*) adds a charmingly informal garden touch to the bouquet and takes some of the emphasis away from the more commercial flowers. You will need one bunch (10–12 stems) of iris, seven pink roses, from seven to nine stems of mixed foliage and five stems of flowering currant.

INGREDIENTS

*Flowers and foliage
(see above)*

✤

One reel of very fine wire

✤

*3ft each of two toning
colors of ribbon, 1in wide*

1 Lay out the foliage, with the longest piece in the center and a slightly shorter piece each side. Bind the first few pieces firmly with wire, and add more pieces at an angle, keeping a fan shape so the ingredients do not overlap.

2 Place some irises between the pieces of foliage, cutting them to different lengths. You could use other flowers instead of this combination, but try to maintain a contrast of shapes, with at least one longer or pointed type of flower and something round if you are replacing the roses.

3 The roses can be placed in position next. Bind the wire firmly around one point after each stem or every two or three stems, depending on how confident you feel. Do not lose any of the flowers by burying them in the foliage; in particular, make sure all the roses are visible, as they are the star flowers in the bouquet. Although this example uses only three different types of flower, you could easily produce a beautiful tied bunch using bits and pieces from the garden.

4 Finally, add the flowering currant, which softens the bunch and should be distributed evenly throughout the design. Bind it in firmly and then cut the wire and tuck it into the bunch. Cover the wire by tying the two ribbons simultaneously around the bunch at the point where you have been binding. Make a large bow, and then cut the ends of the ribbon at an angle.

A circular arrangement

This would make a delightful table center or could be placed on a coffee table or hearth. The ingredients are simple and inexpensive, but the end result is charming. The arrangement is made with wet florist's foam, so it is also long lasting.

$\mathscr{A}$ circular arrangement

This natural design, reminiscent of woodland glades or streams, would be ideal as a table center as it is so low. The ring of florist's foam is available from florists' or other craft stores and comes in a plastic dish, so it needs no other base. You could use any type of moss; the varieties used here are bun moss and reindeer moss, but all types would be suitable. Moss can be dried and then resuscitated, becoming bright green again very easily. The stones could be replaced by small shells or cones, and obviously any other flowers could be substituted for the white daisies. I have used two stems of white single chrysanthemums, a large sprig of eucalyptus, some prostrate juniper, and the two varieties of moss.

INGREDIENTS

Flowers and foliage,
see above

Moss (two types used here)

Stones

22 gauge stub wires,
in 3in lengths

Green florist's foam ring,
10in in diameter

1 Soak the foam well, holding it under the tap. Bend the wires into hairpin shapes. Using flexible pieces of moss to cover the inner foam, hairpin the moss to the foam. Cover the ring with the mosses and stones, leaving spaces for flowers.

2 Continue around the ring, inserting the juniper by pushing small stems into the foam. Add the eucalyptus, either at an angle or straight in like the juniper.

3 Cut the chrysanthemum stems very short – about 2in long – and place them around the ring. Remember to decorate the outer edge of the foam, as this will be seen as much as the top. A smaller version could be made using small clumps of lawn daisies.

$\mathscr{A}$ basket for a bedroom

A basket of flowers looks wonderful anywhere in the house, but seems particularly welcoming in a bedroom. If this color scheme does not match your decor, you could substitute cream orchids and change the colors of the other flowers. As it is made with wet florist's foam, this arrangement should last well, providing you have conditioned the foliage and flowers carefully before using them. You will need from 20 to 30 pieces of assorted foliage, about 6in long; I have used silvery *Atriplex halimus*, *Vibernum tinus* 'Variegata' and eucalyptus. The flowers in the basket are a bunch of yellow and red Singapore orchids, a small bunch of yellow Peruvian lilies (*Alstroemeria*) and ten apricot roses.

INGREDIENTS

Flowers and foliage,
see above

❧

A half block of green
florist's foam

❧

A basket, about 8in
in diameter

1 If unlined, line the basket with plastic. Soak the foam and place it in the basket. Insert the foliage evenly, hiding most of the foam and putting some shorter pieces at the top. Add the orchids, breaking sprays into individual flowers.

2 Add the alstroemeria, again using separate flowers rather than whole sprays. Finish with the apricot roses, trimming the stems to about 4–5in and removing any leaves and thorns.

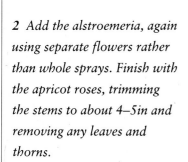

Rose tree & Garden posy

This lovely tree is a very unusual way to present roses for a birthday or any other occasion. They are in fresh flower foam so they will last well and look delightful. The posy is very simple to make and would be ideal as a gift for a friend or hostess.

Rose tree

The clear pink roses are here prettily paired with some unsophisticated feverfew daisies, and the result is a charming tree that would make an unusual gift or treat – perhaps from you to yourself. You will need two dozen spray roses, a bunch of fresh sweet bay, and a large bunch of feverfew. To make the tree base: first, if there is a hole in the terracotta pot, cover it with cardboard; fill the pot up to two-thirds with cement; when the mixture has stiffened a little, insert a stick, approximately 16in high, to act as the trunk, and leave to dry for two to three days.

INGREDIENTS

Flowers and leaves
(see above)

❧

Tree base in a 5in
terracotta pot

❧

One block of green
florist's foam

❧

One green florist's foam
ball, 3¹/₂in in diameter

❧

2yds of ribbon,
¹/₄in wide

❧

26 gauge florist's wires

❧

1 Soak the foam, then cut the block to cover the cement; it should lie level with the rim of the pot. Push the ball onto the 'trunk'. Cover the ball and the foam base with sweet bay sprigs. Cut the ribbon in half; form each length into loops, secured with wire, and insert one into the ball, near the trunk, and the other into the base.

2 *Wire small bunches of feverfew, trimming the stems to about 2–3in. Place the bunches around the tree and the base, taking care to achieve an even coverage with the daisy-like flowers.*

3 *Separate the sprays of roses into individual stems, trimming each stem to the same length as the feverfew. Place the roses into the arrangement, again making sure that you have an even coverage, and also making a final check all around to ensure that no foam is visible when you have finished.*

Garden posy

A few flowers can quickly be turned into a very attractive gift by presenting them in a pretty posy frill. Providing you keep all the stalks to a similar length, the posy can be put into a vase once it has been received. You will need a small bunch of 'Doris' pinks, three or four sprays of roses, seven scented geranium leaves, and a small bunch of broom.

INGREDIENTS

Flowers and leaves
(see above)

❧

A cream or white posy frill,
8in in diameter

❧

A reel of very fine wire

❧

3ft of ribbon, 1in wide,
to tone with the colours in
the posy

1 First take three pinks and then the scented geranium leaves; bind these together in a bunch, and then bind in some broom. As you add materials, keep the wire in one place on the bunch rather than letting it travel up and down the stalks.

2 *Add in the spray roses and keep binding, moderately tightly, in the same position. If you pull too hard on the wire, you will cut the stems, but if the wire is too loose, the posy will fall apart, so aim for a happy medium!*

3 *Continue to bind in the ingredients: add some more 'Doris' pinks, then look at the shape of the circle and take in extra materials, choosing whatever you consider necessary to keep the shape. Finally, push the posy frill up the stems until you can push no further, and tie the ribbon as tightly as possible around the base of the posy frill, to hold it in position. Tie the ends of the ribbon into a bow.*

47

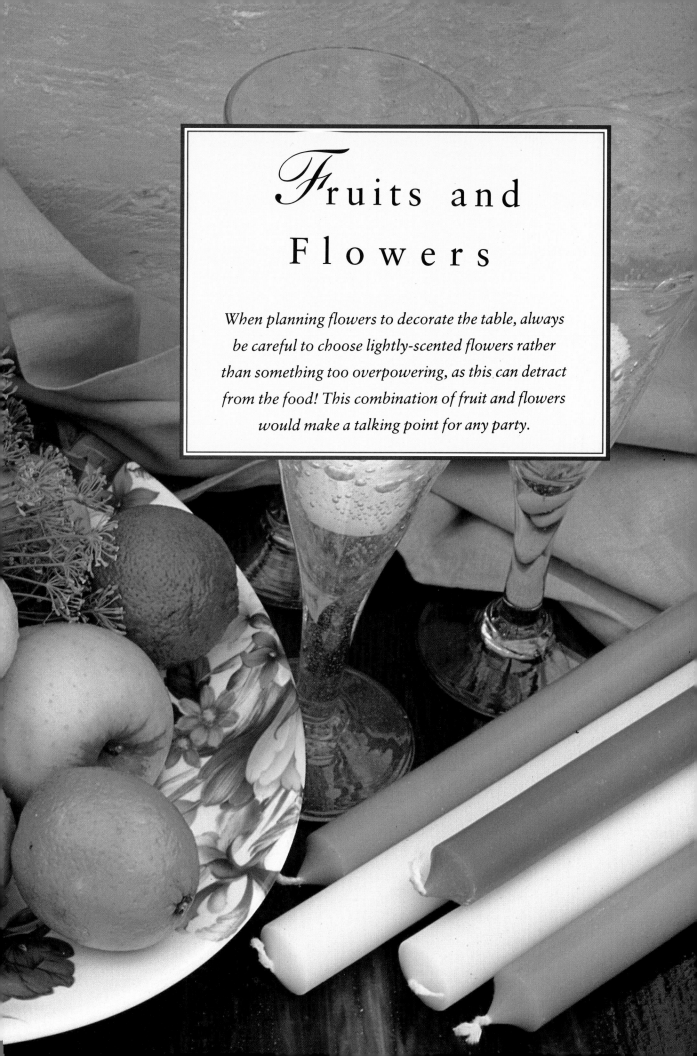

Fruits and Flowers

When planning flowers to decorate the table, always be careful to choose lightly-scented flowers rather than something too overpowering, as this can detract from the food! This combination of fruit and flowers would make a talking point for any party.

Fruits and Flowers

Using fresh lemons and limes adds an exciting novelty to the arrangement. The aromatic herbal greenery blends together to make a soft greeny-gray foil to the bright yellow of the fruit and flowers. Six apples, two lemons and four limes were used here, but there is an ever-increasing range of exotic fruits now on offer, and you might have fun experimenting with other ingredients, such as star fruit, green tomatoes or small yellow bell peppers, always aiming for an attractive balance of scent, colour and form.

INGREDIENTS

Fruits (see above)

◈

*Seven large pale
yellow roses*

◈

*Herbs – one small bunch of
tansy leaves and one of rue
('Jackman's Blue'), and a
bunch of dill flowers*

◈

Shallow oval serving dish

◈

*Quarter block of green
florist's foam*

*1 Put the dill and the roses in
a bucket of water until needed
to make sure that the flowers
do not wilt. Soak the foam in
water and then place it in the
middle of the serving dish.
Cover a diagonal stripe of the
foam with foliage – this could
be any herbal greenery of a
muted greeny gray.*

*2 Put the fruit into position,
making sure you have the*   *same number of each variety
at each side of the arrangement.*

50

3 Cut the stems of the dill fairly short – about 1½–2in – and disperse it among the foliage, keeping the diagonal effect running across the foam block.

4 Finally, insert the roses in the arrangement. As with the dill flowers, the roses will last much longer if they have been given plenty of water before they are used. Possible substitutes for the roses include yellow lilies, pale yellow tulips, or perhaps white roses.

Conditioning flowers and foliage

The first and most important point, whether you are gathering the flowers and foliage from your garden or purchasing them from a florist, is to treat them correctly to prolong their life as much as possible. If you are buying flowers from a good florist, they should be well conditioned already, but it is better to be safe than sorry.

Flowers should all be cleanly cut with a sharp pair of scissors, rather than sawn or tugged at with fingers or a blunt knife. Do not crush the stems of flowers as this merely damages them and prevents them from drinking water – a clean cut will work much more effectively. Although this is not always possible, it is preferable to cut the stem under water, the reason being that this will stop any air bubbles from travelling up the stem and preventing a good flow of water. In practice, however, I usually cut the stems quickly and get them under water as soon as possible. Cut the stems at an angle to help them drink the water; if a stem is cut flat and the cut end touches the bottom of the vase, this will limit the amount of water that can be taken up.

Once the stems have been cut at an angle and any surplus foliage removed, they should be placed in deep water so that they can have a long drink before being placed in a vase. If, however, you are going to put them in a simple arrangement that will allow them free access to plenty of water, then you could skip this step. Foliage and flowers cut from the garden should definitely be placed in deep water and preferably left for several hours; I would leave foliage overnight.

FLOWER FOOD

There is no need to use an expensive flower food – if the florist gives you some with the flowers, then by all means use it, but otherwise you can make your own mixture. Fill half the vase with lemonade and half with fresh water, then add one drop of household bleach. This will prevent any build up of bacteria in the vase, and the sugar in the lemonade will feed the flowers. There are many suggestions for flower food, but this mixture seems to work well with many varieties and helps to prolong their life. If you have particularly long-lasting flowers, which seem happy to go into a second week on display, change the water after five days and cut the stems again; this will enable the flowers to continue drinking the water and food efficiently.

EQUIPMENT

There are a few pieces of equipment that are useful when arranging fresh flowers, although a small collection of vases is basically sufficient. Florist's foam is widely available and makes flower arranging so much easier. If you use foam in an arrangement, or an arrangement is delivered to you from a florist in foam, then keep replenishing the water regularly as it will dry out quite rapidly. Wires in varying thicknesses are useful, especially a small reel of fine, silver-colored wire.

Individual accessories will depend upon the project you want to undertake, and in this book they are all listed where necessary. It is worth collecting a small store of useful accessories as and

Collect useful odds and ends for flower arranging gradually, as and when you see them.

when you see them, for instance while visiting a garden center or craft store. If you have a box of 'useful' things, you will be spared from making a special journey when you want to try a new type of arrangement. Candleholders, for example, are well worth buying. They are not expensive; they can be used many times, and they will hold candles safely and securely in either fresh or dried arrangements. (Leaning candles can spoil a display, as they catch the eye more than the flowers.)

Baskets and jugs are another item that can be collected whenever you find a good source. Unfortunately, a good basket collection may pose storage problems, but small containers in general are always useful and take up less space.

Flowers from a florist are obviously quite an expense if bought on a regular basis. Growing them in the garden is a wonderful alternative. However, I often find that keen gardeners will not

pick flowers for the house and prefer to leave them in the garden, which leads you back to square one. My suggestion would be to have a few flowers that are for cutting, but to concentrate on growing various types of foliage in the garden for use in arrangements. It is very difficult to obtain any selection of greenery at all from most florists, apart from ferns, eucalyptus and one or two other options.

If you have a good selection of foliage in your garden, you will be able to spend a reasonable sum buying a few choice flowers and fill your arrangements with many lovely and unusual pieces of greenery. An arrangement containing only a selection of foliage can look truly beautiful, and you may prefer this type of design at times!

Chapter 2
$\mathcal{U}$sing Scented
Flowers

The beautiful shapes and colors of flowers, combined with their delicacy and freshness, can be uplifting and a wonderful tonic, but the memory that lingers is often the smell – the heady perfume of old-fashioned roses in the summer air, the exciting spices of Christmas, or the joyful fresh springtime scents of narcissi and hyacinths – for these can be powerful reminders of times past and special people in your life.

Adding perfume to a flower arrangement gives it another dimension, and making your own pot pourri can prove a very interesting and relaxing pastime. Lavender and other herbs will always be among my favorite plants, for these have a subtle but lingering perfume. The following projects are designed to inspire and persuade you to try your hand at something new. Working with essential oils is fascinating, and whether the arrangement that catches your eye is a fresh display or pot pourri, I hope you will enjoy experimenting with these ideas.

Lavender & roses

This dried arrangement combines two of my favorite fragrant flowers, the blue of the lavender making a lovely contrast to the soft pink roses. Their gentle fragrance can be heightened by using some lavender or rose oil on the finished arrangement.

Lavender & roses

This very special arrangement is simple to make but includes some luxurious ingredients that will make it a basket to be treasured. There are many varieties of lavender; this is an English type – *Lavandula spica* – which is easily grown in the garden. The roses are two commercially-grown varieties, which could be bought fresh and dried at home. I have used four large bunches of lavender and forty roses, twenty of each variety. The other flowers are a bunch of dried asters, which add a dainty touch to the arrangement.

INGREDIENTS

A medium-sized basket with a base approximately 10in in diameter

෨

One block of dry florist's foam, one pronged foam attachment and glue

෨

Dried lavender, roses and asters

෨

Four lace-edged handkerchiefs in cream or white

1 Glue the pronged attachment to the base of the basket and press the foam block on top, trimming the foam to fit. Separate the lavender into bundles of nine or ten stalks and, using all four bunches, fill the basket evenly.

2 Strip all the leaves from the rose stems; cut them to a suitable length, and then insert them among the lavender, one by one. The roses can be spread evenly among the lavender or placed in small groups of three or five flowers together. The colour scheme of the basket could easily be altered by changing the varieties of rose.

3 Add some small bunches of the asters to lighten the arrangement. Make sure that they are not longer than the lavender, or they will overshadow this very important ingredient. Finally, tuck the lace-edged handkerchiefs into the basket placing one at each side of the handle.

Rose pot pourri & Herbal wreath

Making your own pot pourri creates a mixture that bears no resemblance to any commercial blends, and possesses infinitely prettier color and fragrance. A fresh herbal wreath is also unlikely to be available commercially.

Rose pot pourri

The color scheme of this pot pourri is rose pink, creamy white and green, but the basic instructions can be used with any combination of ingredients. Your own pot pourri mixture will be far more interesting than any commercially-produced pot pourri and you can choose your own fragrance or just rely on the natural fragrance of the roses. This blend contains approximately a cupful of each of the following dried ingredients: small red roses, pink roses, small green leaves (boxwood or privet work quite well), pink peony petals and white larkspur. You should choose something spectacular to decorate the top; I have used two small peonies.

INGREDIENTS

*Dried flowers and petals
(see above)*

*¼oz of orris root
powder (optional)*

*40–50 drops of perfume oil
or essential oil of your
choice (here, 25 drops rose
oil, 15 lavender oil and 5
clove oil; one teaspoon
holds about 60 drops)*

*Ceramic or glass bowl for
mixing*

*Large plastic bag
with tie*

1 Prepare your dried materials (see pages 6–7). Measure very roughly one cup of each of the petal and leaf ingredients into a ceramic bowl. You can easily alter the mixture according to what is available in your garden; most combinations will work.

2 Add the oil to the ingredients first, counting the drops, and then add the powdered orris root. Using a metal spoon, stir and fold in the oil and orris root very gently, taking great care not to damage or break up too many of the flowers and other ingredients. If you do not want to add the orris root then it can be omitted, but the strength of the perfume will be weakened and the pot pourri will not smell strongly for very long. The orris root acts as a fixative for the oil and keeps the scent within the mixture for much longer.

3 Empty the bowl into a large plastic bag and tie the neck tightly. Keep it in a cupboard or other dark place for a week or two to enable the fragrances to blend together and mature. Shake or stir the ingredients regularly, to distribute the oils evenly. If you are not happy with the perfume after a week or so, more drops can be added to alter the composition of the fragrance and the mixture can then be returned to the bag for another week or two. Finally, display the pot pourri in an open bowl and decorate the top with some special flowers, such as the air-dried peonies seen here.

Herbal wreath

This wonderful herbal wreath would look stunning in a kitchen and has a secondary use as a source of dried herbs. You can make the wreath with fresh herbs and allow them to dry naturally, or you could dry the herbs in a microwave first and then attach them to the ring. The components of the ring can vary according to the plants that are easily at hand. Herbs are available in supermarkets, fruit and vegetable stores and many other sources now, so it should not be too difficult to obtain some even if you don't grow them yourself. You will need six fairly large bunches of herbs. I have used parsley, rosemary, sweet bay leaves, mint, lavender and thyme.

INGREDIENTS

Six bunches of herbs (see above)

One vine or willow ring, with a diameter of approximately 10in

22 gauge florists' wires, for bunching

A glue gun and glue

1 First attach some of the sweet bay leaves – I have used fresh leaves but you could easily use ready dried ones. Then position the rosemary; this dries beautifully on the wreath, so there is no need to dry it beforehand. The stems can either be wired together in bunches or glued on individually.

2 *Continue to build the design around the ring by adding the mint, wired in medium-sized clumps. These can be attached fresh or dried. The lavender is also wired into bunches; I have used dried lavender but either fresh or dried is suitable, providing the lavender is in flower at the time you wish to make the wreath. Try to get an even shape all around the ring, with a reasonably thick covering of ingredients, so that the components like mint and thyme do not look too thin when they dry, leaving gaps in the ring.*

3 *Add the last two ingredients – the thyme and parsley. I have used both of these fresh as they become a little brittle when dried. Bunch them both thickly to compensate for the extent to which they will shrink as they are drying. Other ingredients could be added according to your taste. If you want to decorate the ring with ribbons, these could be added now, or perhaps you might opt for a raffia bow.*

Chilli kitchen wreath

This bright, cheerful ring, with its unexpected combination of spicy aromas, is designed to decorate a kitchen or family room. It is very easily made, being based on a vine or twig wreath and constructed with a glue gun.

Chilli kitchen wreath

Both the chillis and the cinnamon have natural fragrances of their own, but this can be enhanced by adding a little cinnamon oil or another suitable fragrance to the wreath once it is finished. You will need three or four large hydrangea heads, a bunch of 10 red and another of 10 golden/apricot roses, about 15 slices of apple and 20–30 chillis, a few sticks of cinnamon and a spray of red pepper berries. All the ingredients are dried.

INGREDIENTS

Dried materials (see above)

෯

One willow, vine or twig ring, about 12in in diameter

෯

24in of tartan or checked ribbon, 2in wide

෯

12in of matching ribbon, 1in wide

෯

About 6in of 22 gauge florists' wire

෯

A glue gun and glue

෯

1 Form the wider ribbon into a figure of eight, as shown on page 48; wrap the wire firmly around the middle, making a bow, and knot the narrower ribbon over the wire, making two more streamers. Glue the bow to the base of the ring. Separate the hydrangeas into florets and glue these around the ring.

2 Glue three cinnamon sticks across the bow, attaching them one at a time. Further pieces of cinnamon could be included in the design if you wish. Take the apple slices and attach them in groups of three, placing them around the ring. The apple slices can be produced by slicing a fresh apple and drying the slices in a low oven for three or four hours until dry and leathery.

3 Strip the leaves away from the stems of the roses and trim the stems back until they measure about 1–2in. Glue in the rose heads, again in small groups, either keeping the colors separate or mixing them together. Other roses or cheaper flowers could be used to reduce the cost of the project or to change the color scheme. Finally, glue in the chilli peppers one by one; position them in a fairly random fashion around the ring, including some with the group of items on the bow. Add the spray of pepper berries to the bow.

Fruity pot pourri & Perfumed straw hat

This pot pourri mixture is actually made from citrus fruits, berries, apples and cloves, which looks as delicious as it smells! The traditional straw hat is decorated with lovely soft summer peach colors and fragranced with a peach pot pourri oil.

Fruity pot pourri

All the fruit used in this pot pourri is dried in the same way. Slice the fruit fairly thickly; place it on a cake rack in a cool oven, and leave until dry. The apples generally take three to four hours, but the citrus fruit may take longer. The rose hips, pomegranates and apples or oranges studded with cloves were dried over a radiator for about one to two weeks. I have used one of each fruit sliced, three tablespoons of orange rind and three of dried chillies, six to eight broken cinnamon sticks, three cups of small red roses or petals and one of rose hips and dried marigolds. The finished pot pourri is then decorated with peach roses and whole fruits studded with cloves.

INGREDIENTS

Dried fruit and flowers (see above)

❧

½oz of orris root powder (optional)

❧

80-90 drops of essential oil (here, 60 drops sweet orange oil and 30 drops cinnamon; one teaspoon holds about 60 drops)

❧

Ceramic or glass bowl for mixing

❧

Metal spoon

1 Place all the fruit and flower ingredients into the bowl, except the special pieces intended for decoration. If you want to alter the color or texture, now is the time to vary the ingredients or their quantities. Pine cones would go well with this mixture, as would other lumpy seed heads or even nuts.

2 *Count the number of drops required into the bowl; stir gently, using a metal spoon, then add the powdered orris root and stir well, taking great care not to break up any of the ingredients. If you do not require such a long-lasting scent, the orris root can be omitted and the oil stirred into the mix alone. The scent will fade much more quickly, but you can re-oil the mixture, using the same technique, once the perfume is too faint.*

3 *Tip the mixture into a large plastic bag and tie firmly at the neck. Place in a warm, dark cupboard and leave for one to two weeks, shaking or stirring the bag regularly to distribute the fragrance and ingredients. This allows the scents to blend and mellow before you place the mixture on display. When it has had a chance to mature, place the pot pourri in a bowl to display it, decorating the top with clove-studded fruits and roses or any other ingredients of your choice.*

$\mathcal{P}$erfumed straw hat

A straw hat can be prettily decorated with preserved summer flowers and transformed into a beautiful creation that could either be enjoyed as an arrangement on the wall or worn on a special occasion. Add some perfume oil to give an extra dimension to this arrangement and to any baskets of dried flowers that you might have in the house, using either a pot pourri reviver oil or a pure essential oil. You will need the following dried materials: 10 pinky peach roses, and 10 golden-apricot roses; one bunch of gypsophila, which is off-white; one bunch of green wheat; one of green amaranthus, and 20 apricot strawflower heads.

INGREDIENTS

Flowers and grasses

❧

One adult-sized straw hat, approximately 16in across, including the brim

❧

3ft each of two ribbons, both 2in wide

❧

One reel of very fine wire

❧

A glue gun and glue

1 Hold the ribbons together, and fold them in a figure of eight (see page 48). Make a bow with long streamers. Make sure the loops are not too large or they will not sit well on the brim of the hat. Glue the bow firmly to the right-angle where the crown meets the brim.

2 Make the wheat into small bunches about 3in long and wire them firmly. Glue these around the hat. Make the amaranthus into bunches of a similar size and add these to the wheat. Next, make the gypsophila into neat bunches, again about 2–3in long, and attach these around the brim. Gypsophila air dries very successfully in about a week, either hanging or in a dry bucket.

3 Finally, add the flowers to your design. The roses make a greater impact arranged in groups of three rather than individually dotted around the hat. Likewise the strawflowers, particularly if they have fairly small heads, can be arranged in groups and placed among the wheat and amaranthus. If you are going to hang the hat up on a wall, *hold it up at the correct angle several times to check the effect, rather than keeping it flat on the table the whole time you are adding flowers to the design.*

Bath oil, cologne & Lavender-scented pomander

Making your own bath oil and cologne is amazingly simple and very satisfying. Display the resulting potions in pretty glass perfume bottles and they will look as wonderful as they smell. The lavender-scented pomander is made from a selection of flowers, but has some lavender oil to boost the natural fragrances.

$\mathcal{B}$ath oil and cologne

Making your own cosmetics is one way to ensure that only the best ingredients are used! The bath oil is a simple mixture of almond oil and essential oil, in this case lavender. You can ring the changes by using a different essential oil; you might like to consult an aromatherapy book to find a suitable oil to treat fatigue or depression, to relax or stimulate, to help aches and pains or to concentrate the mind. The fragrance of the cologne is also provided by its essential oil, which can be altered to suit your mood. Lavender oil has many properties, and will help with aches and pains, depression, fatigue and stress-related headaches.

INGREDIENTS

Lavender bath oil:
6tbsp almond oil

৯

1tbsp pure lavender essential oil

৯

Screw-top jar, for mixing

Lavender cologne:
7fl oz distilled water

৯

1tbsp vodka

৯

1tsp pure lavender essential oil

৯

Screw-top jar, for mixing

Lavender bath oil

1 For the bath oil, use a large screw-top jar and mix the almond oil with the lavender oil by screwing down the lid and shaking thoroughly. It is very important to use best quality lavender oil from a reliable source (see page 176).

2 Decant the oil into an attractive container with a tightly fitting lid. If the oil is a gift, add a ribbon bow, *together with a gift tag and brief instructions (add one tablespoon to a bath under fast running water).*

Lavender cologne

1 Mix all the ingredients in a large screw-top jar and, with the lid firmly on, shake very vigorously for a minute or so. As for the bath oil, make sure you use the very best quality lavender oil for this cologne.

2 Decant the mixture into an attractive bottle, preferably with a ground glass stopper, and label with a ribboned gift tag. An old alternative recipe uses dry white wine (still, not sparkling) instead of the water and vodka; this produces a different but interesting result. This cologne can either be added to bathwater or applied neat to the skin; it feels wonderful in the heat of summer if it is kept in the refrigerator.

Lavender-scented pomander

When space is at a premium and there is little room for dried flowers in baskets or as wall hanging displays, this hanging pomander could be ideal as a decoration. There is a little natural fragrance from the lavender used in making the pomander, but the scent has been enhanced by the addition of some lavender oil sprinkled onto the flowers after the pomander was finished. You will need a small bunch of sea lavender, which in this example has been dyed a pale lavender blue, one bunch of medium-sized poppy seed heads, one of echinops, one bunch of English or French lavender, a bunch of brunia (an exotic seed head), and 30 cream strawflower heads.

INGREDIENTS

Dried flowers and seed heads (see above)

❧

Approximately 3ft of cord, for hanging (the length can be longer or shorter, as desired)

❧

20in of ribbon, 1in wide, for bows at the top of the sphere

❧

Dry florist's foam sphere, 3½in in diameter

❧

22 gauge florists' wires

1 Fold the cord in half and wind a wire firmly around the two cut ends, leaving a long leg. Push this through the foam ball, burying the cord ends. Trim the projecting wire to about ½–1in; bend it back on itself, and bury it in the foam. Make two bows from the ribbon (see page 93) and glue one to each side of the base of the loop.

2 *Cover the ball with the sea lavender. Do not cover it too thickly or there will be no room for the other ingredients, but also beware using too little material and thus leaving gaps through which the foam will be visible. Next, start adding the poppy heads and echinops. They can either be pushed in at random or placed in groups, according to your taste. Use the smaller echinops in the bunch as some heads may be too large and would overshadow the other ingredients.*

3 *Place some of the brunia in the ball, dividing it into small clusters rather than trying to use whole stems. The strawflower heads can be placed in next; you can either glue the heads in position or, as in this case, use wired strawflowers, which slide into the foam easily. Finally, divide the lavender into small bunches; wire each bunch firmly but gently, and distribute the bunches throughout the ball. If you want the ball to smell more strongly of lavender, drop some lavender essential oil onto the flowers and seed heads and leave it to soak in.*

Fragrant flowers in terracotta

If you have scented flowers or plants in your garden you can arrange something lovely in the house very easily. Even if you have to add to the quantity with a few flowers bought from the florist this still makes an arrangement a relatively inexpensive way of giving yourself a great deal of pleasure.

Fragrant flowers in terracotta

A simple group of flowers arranged in a selection of containers can look strikingly effective, yet couldn't be simpler to arrange. The terracotta containers used here have been painted to tone with their surroundings. Here, I have used a medley of highly scented flowers – a bunch of lilies of the valley, some stephanotis, lilac and phlox.

INGREDIENTS

Flowers (see above)

৵

*A selection of containers –
here, two vases 8in high,
one bowl 7in in diameter,
a couple of small flowerpots
3in in diameter*

৵

Six or seven small sea shells

1 Arrange the taller ingredients in the larger vases. Make sure they have plenty of water, and cut the stems on a slant to make sure that the stems do not touch the base of the container, preventing water from passing up the stalks.

2 Position a few shells on the base of the bowl and fill the bowl with water. Place the stephanotis in the water – some heads together and some individually. The individual heads will only float facing upwards if you shorten the length of the flower trumpet; without this, they will turn on their sides.

3 Seal the holes in the small flowerpots and stack them one inside another to give more height. Fill the top pot with water and place the bunch of lilies of the valley and some leaves inside the flowerpot. The mixed perfumes of these highly scented flowers are quite delicious!

Scented flower basics

Smells or fragrances are very much a matter of personal taste, and what suits one person may not be the choice of another. However, the natural smells of flowers are usually widely acceptable; they are often light and subtle, with a pretty fragrance that can waft through the house if you place the flowers in a spot where you will pass them frequently.

Growing Fragrant Flowers

There are many plants that can be included in a garden to add perfume to a summer's evening or sweet scents to a vase of flowers. The first flower that comes to mind must be the rose. The perfume of a rose is legendary and has been prized for hundreds of years. Sadly, many roses are now bred for their blooms and less importance is given to their scent. There are still, however, many varieties that will give a magnificent perfume, such as the Bourbon rose 'Madame Isaac Pereire', or the *rugosa* variety 'Frau Dagmar Hastrup'. Many other roses have a fragrance, and it is worth seeking out old roses and planting them with a mixture of aromatic herbs such as rue, mint, rosemary and lemon balm to make a stroll in the garden even more pleasurable.

Herbs are another collection of plants that are simple to grow and work very hard for the amount of space they are allocated in the garden. Once you have established a bed of herbs, you will find endless uses for them, both in the kitchen and for decorative and medicinal purposes. A large clump of lavender by the back door may be reminiscent of the old cottage gardens but smells just as wonderful as you go in and out, if your home is a modern house or first floor apartment.

If you enjoy having flowers in the house, then why not plan your garden with that thought in mind? If you put together several flowering species that bloom at the same time, there may be a noticeable gap when you pick them to fill a vase. Try to plant carefully, so that there are several items with attractive foliage mixed with the star flowering plants; with planning, cutting for the house will leave the garden unspoilt. In this way, you will be able to enjoy the colors and scents of garden flowers indoors, without offending a garden-loving partner.

Drying and Preserving Scents

There are several ways to add perfume to your home; the obvious one is to use fresh flowers and foliage to decorate the house. In these days of central heating, however, fresh arrangements can be very short lived, and dried flowers or pot pourri can give wonderful aromas to all parts of the home.

Although it is now easier to purchase dried flowers and ingredients for pot pourri, nothing compares with the satisfaction of growing your own materials in the garden and drying them. Producing your finished arrangements from seed is very pleasing and reduces the cost considerably.

Air Drying Flowers

A wide selection of garden and shop-bought flowers can easily and successfully be air dried at home (see page 130), and you can add a few drops of essential or pot pourri oil, as described below, to a finished arrangement to enhance the scent.

DRYING INGREDIENTS IN THE MICROWAVE

Drying plant materials in the microwave for use in pot pourri is quick and can be great fun, as you achieve instant results. This method, however, is not suitable for larger flowers or indeed for materials to be used in arrangements, as the finished shapes are not good enough.

To dry pieces of herbs or flower heads for use in pot pourri, take a couple of sheets of paper towel and use this as a base. Lay the sprigs of herb on the paper and place into the microwave. Use medium-to-full heat and cook for between 1½ and 2½ minutes, depending on the size and amount of plant material in the oven. Once the herbs feel dry, remove them from the oven and allow them to cool for five or ten minutes. Experiment with your particular model as times and temperatures vary from oven to oven. Many items can be dried in this way – scented rose petals, for example – but whole flowers will lose their shape and be suitable only for pot pourri.

Another option is to use essential oils to add perfume. These are extracted from fruits, leaves, flowers and barks, and contain no added chemical only the natural oil from the plant.

They are consequently very different from the mixed perfume oils and chemical fragrances that are sold as pot pourri reviver oils. The latter are perfectly acceptable for use in pot pourri work, or for scenting dried flower arrangements, but I would recommend using essential oils in any skin preparations, such as lavender bath oil or cologne.

Essential oils are available from some drug stores and health food stores as well as the sources mentioned at the end of the book; they open up a whole new world of scents, and it can be very absorbing to experiment with new fragrances and combinations.

Chapter 3

Designs with Dried Flowers

Beautiful dried flower arrangements add a stunning touch of color to a dark corner or provide a focal point in a fireplace or on a table. Dried and preserved flowers also last for months, as opposed to days or weeks for fresh flowers, so once you have put some effort into an arrangement you will be able to enjoy the benefits for ages.

The way to get the best value out of dried flowers is to grow and arrange them yourself. If you have a garden in which you can spare a little room, then a couple of varieties of flower can form the basis of a collection that may either be sufficient for simple arrangements or can be supplemented with purchased materials. The section on pages 130-31 describes two easy ways of preserving your crop of flowers and leaves.

Several types of arrangement are demonstrated here, and I hope you will enjoy using them and also adapting the designs by varying the materials and colors to suit your individual needs.

A basket of garden flowers

All the wonderful flowers used in this basket can be grown in the garden. Peonies and roses are often expensive to buy, but home-grown specimens can be dried in the house with surprising ease.

${\mathscr{A}}$ basket of garden flowers

Used in this luxurious-looking basket – a lovely reminder of summer to cheer up the winter months – is a collection of hydrangea heads, 15 peonies, two bunches of small cream roses, a bunch of *Atriplex hortensis*, pink and white larkspur (easily grown from seed), and a small bundle of honesty (*Lunaria*) seed heads. The latter are very useful in fresh arrangements when in their early stage, before the seeds are fully developed, and it is a delight to find that they dry so beautifully, retaining their attractive green color to perfection.

INGREDIENTS

Large basket, with a base measuring approximately 10in in diameter

❧

Two blocks of dry florist's foam

❧

Two pronged foam attachments

❧

Dried flowers and seed heads (see above)

❧

Approximately 3ft each of pale pink and white ribbon, 1in wide, with two 22 gauge florists' wires

1 Glue the pronged attachments to the base of the basket and press the foam blocks on top of them. Cover the foam with hydrangea heads, then add the atriplex and the pink larkspur (trim the stalks – if you leave them too long, the arrangement will be too large and the basket handle will be hidden).

2 Now place the cream or white larkspur throughout the arrangement. The peonies can first be made to look a little larger by steaming them gently over a boiling kettle. Distribute them evenly throughout the arrangement, then add the honesty seed heads in the spaces between the peonies.

3 To finish the arrangement, position the small cream roses at random. Cut each ribbon in two and, taking a length of each color, form looped bows as shown below, binding the loops with wire, and leaving ends of wire to attach the bows to the arrangement. This is the method used for all the bows in the book.

Forming a ribbon bow

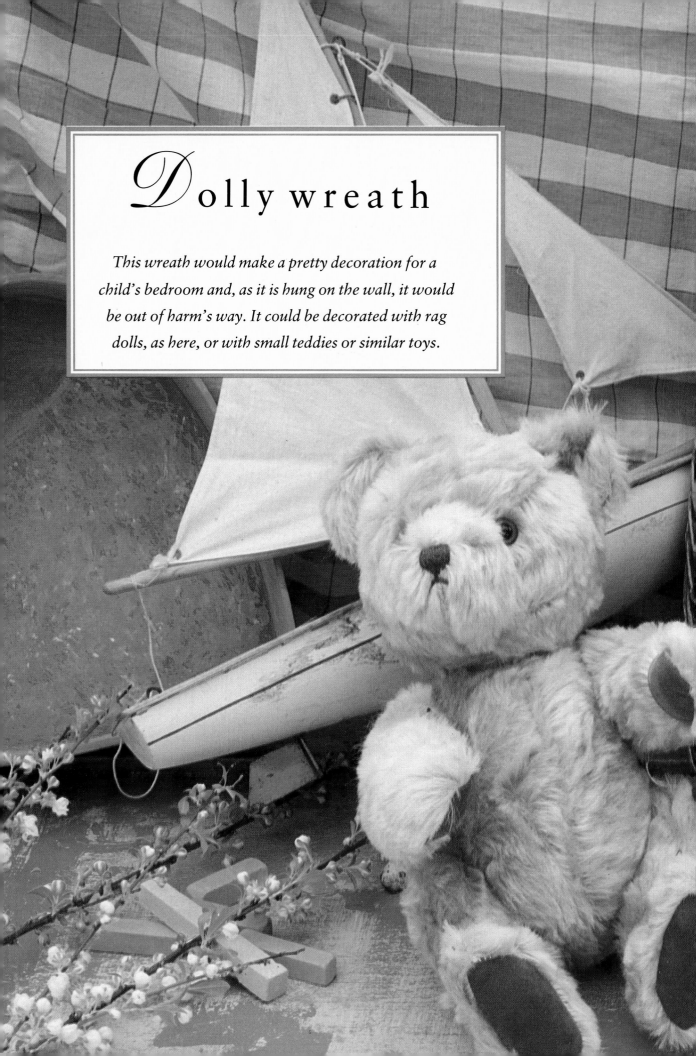

Dolly wreath

This wreath would make a pretty decoration for a child's bedroom and, as it is hung on the wall, it would be out of harm's way. It could be decorated with rag dolls, as here, or with small teddies or similar toys.

Dolly wreath

Twig or cane rings of this type can be purchased from most florists. A small mixed bunch of pink and blue larkspur, a little of either broom bloom or gypsophila (whichever is available), some pink roses and a few sprays of eucalyptus are all the dried materials you will need for this pretty ornament. Small children tend to chew anything they can get hold of, so make sure that it is hung well out of reach, and if you substitute other materials for those used here, check that there is nothing poisonous that might fall to the floor and be eaten.

INGREDIENTS

Twig or cane ring,
8-10in in diameter

Dried flowers and leaves
(see above)

Two small rag dolls, or
other small toys

9ft of matching ribbon,
¼in wide for bows
(optional), with one
22 gauge florists' wire for
each bow

Glue and glue gun

1 Using a hot glue gun, attach sprays of eucalyptus around two-thirds of the ring, leaving room for the flowers and dolls in the central position. Secure the dolls with plenty of glue, positioning them so that they appear to sit sideways on the ring, rather than staring straight out.

2 Cut the larkspur quite short and glue the stems in place on the ring, mixing blue and pink flowers at random to avoid a regimented effect. Make sure that the larkspur is trimmed sufficiently short – if it is much longer than the eucalyptus this will spoil the finished effect.

3 Still using the glue gun, secure the roses in position one by one, carefully placing them in the remaining gaps in the design. They look attractive either placed in small groups of three or singly. Finally, add a few touches of broom bloom or gypsophila. Whichever you use, it must be cut very short or the ring may look untidy when you have finished. As an optional finishing touch, you might like to add a ribbon bow with streamers (see page 11 for the basic method, but form streamers as well as loops).

$\mathcal{A}$ kitchen wall basket

An attractive collection of herbs, spices and preserved bread rolls makes a marvellous conversation piece in a kitchen. It is arranged in a flat-backed basket so that it can hang out of the way of the work surfaces.

$\mathscr{A}$ kitchen wall basket

The bread rolls used in this arrangement are preserved by drying them slowly in the bottom of a cool oven for several hours until they feel very light. Once the rolls have cooled, spray them all over with a matt varnish to protect them from insects. The dried materials that are added to the rolls and cinnamon to make up this unusual wall basket are hydrangeas, marjoram, oregano and natural wheat, together with atriplex. When choosing a position for your wall basket, make sure that it is away from the main cooking area – excessive dampness can cause mildew.

INGREDIENTS

A flat-backed wall basket, with a pouch measuring approximately 8in × 6in at the base

Half a block of florist's foam

Five each of bread rolls, cinnamon sticks, and very heavy gauge florist's wires

Dried materials (see above)

4ft 6in of terracotta-colored ribbon, 1in wide, for bows (optional), with two 22 gauge florist's wires

1 Glue the foam into the basket and cover it with hydrangea heads. Spread the wheat throughout the basket, using most of a large bunch, to give good colour and to fill the basket. Use the wheat fairly short or you will obscure most of the basket once the arrangement is finished.

2 Push a thick wire into each of the bread rolls and, if necessary, glue the wires into the rolls. Next, place the rolls evenly through the arrangement. Add some cinnamon sticks by pushing the ends into the foam. Use a small bunch of atriplex to help to fill the basket and to add touches of stronger color.

3 Finish the basket by adding the marjoram and oregano – both of which not only contribute wonderful colors to the basket, but a lovely herbal scent as well. Terracotta-colored ribbons can be formed into two bows, one at each side of the basket (see page 93).

Golden wedding ring & Table centerpiece

Either of these, or both together, would make a delightful gift for a golden wedding celebration. These arrangements are very versatile and, with minor changes in color, could be adapted to suit numerous occasions.

Golden wedding ring

Unusual golden wedding presents are hard to find, and this ring will please on two counts – it is beautiful to look at, and you will have the additional pleasure of making it yourself. The roses used here were the variety 'Calypso', but any golden shade, or even a cream, would be suitable. Two bunches of the roses were combined with one bunch of *Achillea filipendula*, one of cream strawflowers and glycerined beech leaves. The dried materials are attached with a hot glue gun, in the same way as those used for the Dolly wreath (see page 94).

INGREDIENTS

Dark twig ring, 12-14in in diameter

Dried materials (see above)

3ft each of cream and gold ribbon, 1in wide, for bows (optional), with two 22 gauge florist's wires

Glue and glue gun

1 Using a hot glue gun, attach some sprigs of beech leaves in position, covering about two-thirds of the ring. Make loops with tails from both colors of ribbon; wire them (see page 93), and then glue them just left of center, on the base of the ring.

2 *Add the achillea flowers, cutting off the stems so that you are attaching just the main head of each flower. Place them evenly around the ring – if you cluster them too close together there will not be enough room for the roses and strawflowers.*

3 *Next, attach the strawflowers, again distributing them in a random fashion around the ring, without crowding any too close together. When these are in place, attach the roses one at a time, making sure that each is firmly glued in place. The roses can be placed in small groups or individually.*

Table centerpiece

Although the arrangement shown here has gold candles in it, you could easily substitute another color, such as ivory or yellow. This would be an ideal centerpiece for a golden wedding celebration, but it could equally well be used for Christmas or any other festive occasion. Never leave the arrangement unattended when the candles are lit; like all dried materials, those used here – eucalyptus, white *Achillea ptarmica*, cream peonies, yellow roses and *Nigella orientalis* seed heads – are all highly inflammable.

INGREDIENTS

Flat cork base, an oval measuring approximately 9in × 7in

Small piece of dry florist's foam and pronged foam attachment

Two 9in gold candles and candleholders

Dried materials (see above)

6ft of gold ribbon, ½in wide, for bows (optional), with four 22 gauge florist's wires

1 *Glue the pronged foam attachment to the cork base and push the foam onto it. Trim 1in from the candle, and insert the two holders and candles into the foam. Cover the foam with lengths of eucalyptus, taking care to ensure that none of the foam will show. Try to follow the shape of the base, maintaining the oval.*

2 Trim the peonies very short and place these at the centre of the arrangement, spacing them carefully so that they are not all crowded at one side – remember that the arrangement will be viewed from all sides and at a slightly downwards angle when in use. (It is often better to make this type of arrangement from a seated position.) After you have positioned the peonies, distribute the Nigella orientalis *seed heads throughout the arrangement.*

3 Finally, trim the stems of the roses and add them to the arrangement. Also add small clumps of Achillea ptarmica. *Again, distribute both the roses and the achillea evenly throughout the design. Cut the ribbon into four equal pieces and, taking a length for each bow, make four ribbon bows (see page 11) and decorate each side with these.*

Family room arrangement

This attractive arrangement uses various cones, reeds, grasses and dried flowers to achieve a finished effect which is a subtle blend of cream and sepia tones that would suit many different styles of decor.

$\mathcal{F}$amily room arrangement

A large and very stylish arrangement, this combines hydrangea heads, ten cream peonies and the same number of proteas, salignum cones with foliage, and one bunch each of bell reed, foxtail millet and polypogon grass. The materials used are generous in size and the finished effect should be lavish, so you will need to find a basket with a high handle, like the one shown here. Failing that, it would be preferable to have no handle at all, and let the reeds and grasses give the essential height to this elegant arrangement.

INGREDIENTS

Large basket, with a base measuring approximately 8in in diameter

❧

One and a half blocks of dry florist's foam

❧

Pronged foam attachment

❧

Dried materials (see above)

❧

22 gauge florist's wires

❧

3ft of cream ribbon, 1in wide (optional)

1 Glue the pronged foam attachment to the base of the basket and impale the foam block on it. Cut the half block in two and glue the pieces to each side of the main block to help fill the basket evenly. Cover the foam with hydrangea heads, then position the foxtail millet and salignum cones.

2 *Place the cream peonies in position, setting five to each side of the basket handle. Do the same with the proteas, to make sure that the larger ingredients are evenly dispersed. As you work, look at the arrangement from different angles, to check for balance.*

3 *Arrange the bell reed and the grass into small clumps of five or six heads and wire them together (without this, they would be dwarfed by the larger materials). Scatter the clumps throughout the arrangement. Form the ribbon into four bows (see page 11), and place two bows at each side of the basket.*

Pot pourri basket
&
Topiary tree

If you make this pretty tree for yourself, you are likely to be inundated with requests from friends to make one for them. The charming pot pourri basket would be an equally welcome gift.

$\mathcal{P}$ot pourri basket

Pot pourri is a delightful gift in itself, but how much more elegant it is when presented in a charming basket, decorated with dried flowers! The basket is lined with plastic, to prevent the pot pourri from slipping through the gaps. If your basket is not ready-lined, you could line it with paper or fabric. The dried materials comprise pale pink roses, pink-peach statice, pink larkspur, green oregano, marjoram and dyed green statice (*Goniolimon tataricum* var. *angustifolium*, often known as *Statice dumosa*).

INGREDIENTS

Shallow basket, lined, with a base measuring 8in square

Dried flowers (see above)

22 gauge florist's wires

6ft of toning ribbon, ¾in wide, and the same of transparent ribbon

Glue and glue gun

Pot pourri to fill the basket

1 Using the two ribbons together, make two wired bows with the ribbons (see page 11) and glue them to the base of the handles at each side of the basket. Then glue the pink-peach and green statice along the sides of the basket, around the bows.

2 *At this stage, you may decide to continue the design around the entire basket, if you have sufficient materials. The next flower to be added is the pink larkspur. Take care not to keep the larkspur spikes too long, or the final effect will be spidery rather than compact. When the statice and larkspur have been fixed in place, add the marjoram, wiring it into small clumps and attaching these to the basket.*

3 *Finish by filling in the remaining gaps between flowers with the pale pink rosebuds and a small number of tiny wired bunches of green oregano flowers. When the decorations are finished, fill the basket with pot pourri, soaps, chocolates, or whatever else you may have in mind. This basic design is very quick to make and the colors can, of course, be adapted to the filling; a basket for a lemon-scented pot pourri, for example, might be more appropriately edged with yellow statice and cream or deep purple rosebuds.*

Topiary tree

These miniature trees make a very attractive decoration for a hall, living room or bedroom. The dried materials used here were hydrangea heads, *Achillea millefolium* 'Cerise Queen', pink larkspur, dark pink strawflowers and *Nigella orientalis* seed heads. The dried strawflowers can be bought ready-wired or, you can wire them yourself when they are fresh, and dry them wired. For the cement, you can use ordinary building cement, fast-drying cement or plaster-of-Paris.

INGREDIENTS

5in terracotta flower pot

Small quantity of cement, and a straight stick, approximately 16in high

Dry florist's foam ball, 4½in in diameter, and small pieces of foam block

Dried materials (see above)

22 gauge florist's wires or glue and glue gun

3ft each of two shades of pink ribbon, ½in wide

1 If the pot has a hole in the base, cover this with a piece of cardboard. Mix the cement and fill two-thirds of the pot. Once the mixture has stiffened a little, stand the stick in the centre. Leave to dry for two to three days, then impale the ball on the stick. Glue small pieces of foam to the cement, bringing the level to the top of the pot.

2 Cover both the ball and the foam at the base of the stick with hydrangea heads, broken down into smaller pieces.

3 Push in pieces of Achillea *'Cerise Queen' until you have achieved a good covering of both the ball and the base. Next, using fairly short pieces to avoid a straggly effect, add the pink larkspur. Take care to work in the round, stepping back regularly to take a quick look at the overall effect from a distance.*

4 Finally, put in the strawflowers. They can be glued in position, but in this case they were wired. To wire a strawflower, remove the stem, then push the wire up from the back, near the center of the flower; make a small hook at the upper end of the wire, and pull the wire back down, securing the hook in the center of the flower. When you have distributed the helichrysums around the tree, add a good number of Nigella orientalis *seed heads, to give a contrast in both shape and color. Make two wired bows with the ribbon (see page 93), leaving long legs of wire to be pushed well into the foam ball.*

Celebration tree
&
Flowery picnic basket

*These two projects show the versatility of dried flowers –
the tree is a lavish arrangement which would do credit to a
major occasion, such as a wedding, while the hamper has a
quiet rustic charm that would look attractive in virtually
any room.*

Celebration tree

This is a very large version of the tree shown on page 112. It takes a long time to make and you will need to take care to cover the ball well. It is also expensive, but once it is made it will last a long time and give many months – or even years – of pleasure. In addition to the lining of hydrangea heads, the ingredients for this tree included eucalyptus, dyed green statice (*Goniolimon tataricum* var. *angustifolium*, often known as *Statice dumosa*), boxwood foliage, cream peonies, *Achillea ptarmica*, cream strawflowers and poppy seed heads.

INGREDIENTS

*10in flower pot or
similar base*

Broom handle, and cement

*Dry florist's foam ball, 8in
in diameter, and two foam
blocks*

*Dried materials
(see above)*

*18ft of cream ribbon,
1½in wide, with three
22 gauge florist's wires*

Glue and glue gun

1 Cover any hole in the base with card then fill with cement to 2in below the rim. When the cement begins to set, insert the stick, supporting it upright. Leave to dry for three to four days, then impale the ball on the end of the stick. Slice the foam blocks and pack them around the base, level with the rim of the pot.

2 Cover the foam ball and the foam at the base with an even layer of hydrangea heads.

3 Add the green statice in small bunches and the other foliage, in this case eucalyptus and an exotic boxwood. Make sure that the entire ball is evenly covered with greenery.

4 Add the poppy heads and also the cream peonies. To make the peony blooms a little larger and fuller, steam them over a boiling kettle. This softens the flowers slightly so that you can carefully shape them in your hands to make the blooms larger. Finally, add the achillea and glue in the strawflowers. The ribbons can be made into three large loops and tails, wired (see page 93), and then inserted at the same angle as the broom handle. The same flowers and foliage are then added to the base of the tree.

$\mathcal{F}$lowery picnic basket

This small picnic basket would look equally at home in the hall, living room or a bedroom. It has been filled with an unsophisticated selection of materials that are reminiscent of fields in summer. The dried materials seen here are dyed green statice (*Goniolimon tataricum* var. *angustifolium*, often known as *Statice dumosa*), and one bunch each of natural poppy heads, white everlasting daisies (*Helipterum roseum*, also sold as *Acroclinium roseum*), yellow strawflowers, natural wheat and pale and dark blue larkspur. You may, however, wish to vary the flowers and grasses somewhat to suit your own decor while retaining the overall effect.

INGREDIENTS

Picnic-style basket with a base measuring approximately 8in × 6in

❧

Half a block of dry florist's foam

❧

Pronged foam attachment

❧

Dried materials (see above)

❧

3ft each of cream and blue ribbon, 1in wide, with two 22 gauge florist's wires

1 Glue the pronged attachment to the base of the basket and push the foam onto it. Cover the foam with green statice. Add the poppy heads, distributing them evenly at each side of the basket.

2 Add in the wheat, ensuring that it is longer than the statice, but still in proportion to the basket. Use most or all of the bunch – plenty of wheat will help to give an attractive green effect to the arrangement. Next, place the darker blue larkspur in position. Again, make sure there is an equal amount at each side of the basket or one side of the arrangement will look darker than the other.

3 Insert the pale blue larkspur at the same height as the darker blue. Use plenty, to give a good strong blue to the arrangement. Put the white daisies in next, scattering them in small clumps throughout the arrangement. Lastly, place the yellow strawflowers in position. These may either be wired (see page 117, step 4) or attached with a hot glue gun. Wire two ribbon bows (see page 93), using both colors together, and attach a bow to each side of the basket.

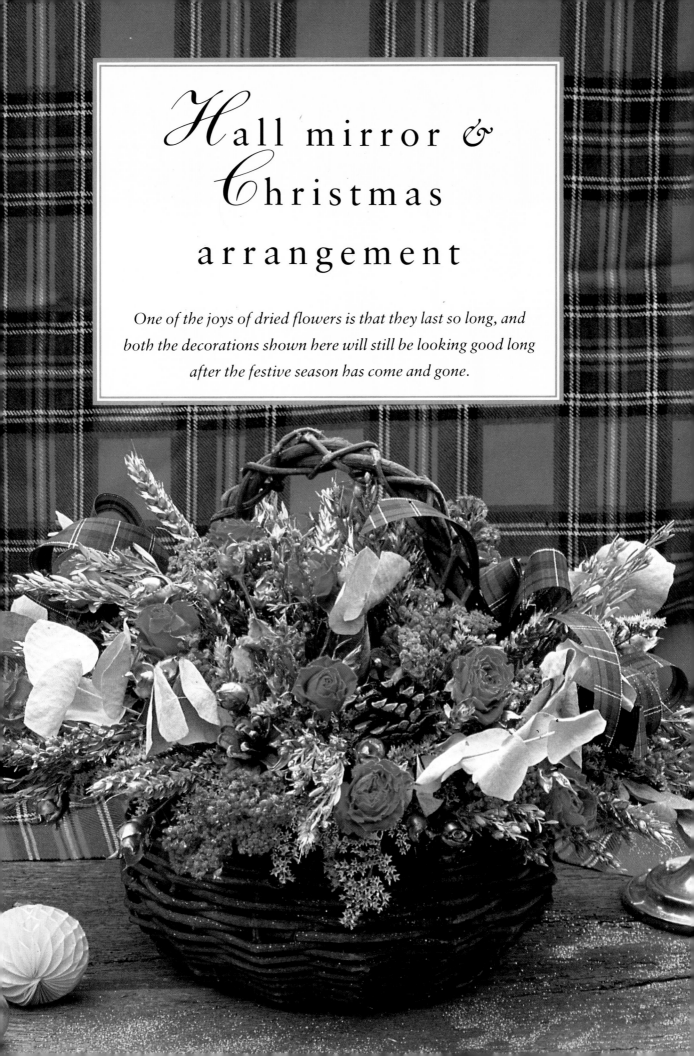

Hall mirror & Christmas arrangement

One of the joys of dried flowers is that they last so long, and both the decorations shown here will still be looking good long after the festive season has come and gone.

$\mathscr{H}$all mirror

The dried materials featured here comprise eucalyptus leaves, crimson roses, larch cones, *Nigella damascena* seed heads, and statice (*Goniolimon tataricum* var. *angustifolium*). They were attached with a hot glue gun – you could use a cold adhesive, but it would be much more difficult. If you feel that the red roses and the cones used here look too Christmassy for a permanent feature like a mirror, you could easily substitute another color of rose and use seed heads in place of the cones. Your local picture framer will make a mirror for you if you cannot find a suitable one.

INGREDIENTS

12in × 10in pine-framed mirror

꧁

Dried materials (see above)

꧁

Glue and glue gun

꧁

Cardboard and clips or household mastic (optional – see step 1)

1 Clean the mirror and place it the correct way up. The materials were glued directly to the mirror shown here. If you do not want to make a permanent feature, you could cut cardboard carrying strips about 7in long and the depth of your frame and attach these to the mirror with clips or household mastic. Glue the statice and eucalyptus in place.

2 Next, place the red roses in position. It is a good idea to lay them all on the mirror and make sure that you are happy with the design before you glue them permanently in situ.

3 Add the larch cones and the nigella seed heads. Try to get a good balance between the top and bottom of the mirror so that you do not get the feeling that one is considerably heavier than the other. Take great care when using the gun not to let any glue drip onto the mirror – it can take a long time to clean mistakes away.

Christmas arrangement

This basket of dried flowers will add a festive touch to a coffee table or create a welcoming atmosphere in the hallway. The dried materials used were statice (*Goniolimon tataricum* var. *angustifolium*), *Achillea millefolium* 'Cerise Queen', gilded salignum foliage, gilded bell reed and gilded wheat, eucalyptus, pine cones and two bunches of red roses.

INGREDIENTS

Dark rustic basket, with a base measuring approximately 6in in diameter

Block of dry florist's foam

Pronged foam attachment

Dried materials (see above)

22 gauge florist's wires

9ft of tartan ribbon, 1in wide

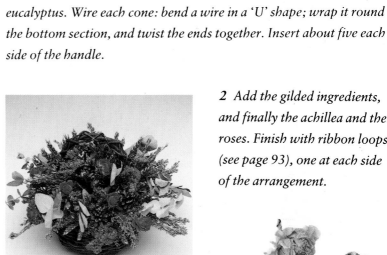

1 Glue the foam in the basket; cover it with statice, and then add the eucalyptus. Wire each cone: bend a wire in a 'U' shape; wrap it round the bottom section, and twist the ends together. Insert about five each side of the handle.

2 Add the gilded ingredients, and finally the achillea and the roses. Finish with ribbon loops (see page 93), one at each side of the arrangement.

Drying flowers

Many of the arrangements in this book are made with materials that you can grow for yourself, even in a relatively small garden, but there are a few basic materials that you will need to buy. Gray or brown florist's foam is manufactured especially for dried flower arranging, and is usually available in bricks, although it is possible to buy foam spheres, cones and circles. Do not purchase the green foam intended for fresh flower arrangements, as this is too crumbly when dry. Another very useful tool is a hot glue gun, available from craft stores. The glue is in the form of opaque sticks, which are fed into the back of the gun and heated. The gun is an economical and efficient tool for many projects, a wide range of household applications.

DRYING FLOWERS AND FOLIAGE

Two methods of preserving flowers are discussed below – air drying and glycerining. The third method by which flowers can be dried at home is by the use of silica crystals or other desiccants. This can produce very lovely results, but it is a more complicated and expensive process, and none of the arrangements in this book include flowers preserved in desiccants. Pick only the best materials for preserving, and make sure that there is no infestation or disease present.

AIR DRYING

The simplest way of preserving flowers is to hang them up and leave them to dry. The flowers should be hung in small bunches and tied with a rubber band to prevent them dropping on the floor, as their stalks shrink while they are drying. Ideally, flowers should be dried in the dark so that they do not lose any color before you use them, but if this is not possible, you can compromise: look for a warm but shady place in the house, where you can spare some space to dry your flowers. The drying bunches can look very decorative, but they can also shed bits and pieces so too many in a kitchen can get very messy!

Many flowers are suitable for air drying, especially the everlasting varieties that are advertised on the packet as being ideal for drying. If you look through a seed catalogue or at a display in the garden center, you are sure to find many ideas for varieties to grow. My favorite flowers to dry are roses. These are simple to dry – just hang up a bunch in a suitable spot; they will dry within a couple of weeks, and many varieties keep their color very well indeed. Dried roses are very expensive to buy, but whether you grow them or buy them fresh, your home-dried roses will be much cheaper and give you tremendous pleasure.

GLYCERINE

This method does not work for flowers, but it is the only way to preserve many varieties of foliage. Beech is a prime example; this cannot be air dried, but when it is glycerined it makes a very useful foliage that lasts for a tremendously long time. It can also be wiped clean when it has become dusty and re-used many times over. Foliage to be preserved in glycerine should be picked when it is mature – usually middle-to-late summer. Choose only perfect leaves, and do not attempt to preserve branches that are too large, or the leaves at the tips will have wilted before the solution reaches them. Strip the bark off the lower stem; crush the stem to help it to take up the mixture, and make sure that you leave as little time as possible between gathering your materials and putting them in the solution.

Glycerine can be bought from a drug store and you need to mix it with an equal quantity of boiling water. Pour this mixture into a tall slim container until you have a depth of about 3in and place the stem of the plant you wish to preserve in the mix. The stem will then take up the glycerine and water mixture and you will be able to see the mix progressing up the stem, since with many foliages there is a marked colour change as the glycerine is taken up. The process takes between six days and three weeks, depending on which variety you are preserving. Once the glycerine has reached the tips of the leaves, remove the stem from the vase; if you leave it too long, the stem will take up too much mixture and beads of glycerine will appear on the surface of the leaves, which can lead to a horrible sticky mess and even mildew.

STORING

Once your flowers have been dried or glycerined, you will probably want to store them for some time before using them. Air-dried flowers may be left hanging where they are, if you have the space; if, however, like most of us, you need the space to dry more flowers, your newly-dried, or glycerined, flowers and foliage can be stored in long florist's boxes. (Your local florist will usually be happy to let you have some.) Make sure that you keep the box tightly closed to prevent anything – moisture, children or insects – from harming your stock.

Roses are generally dried, though the heads may also be preserved in desiccants.

Chapter 4

*P*ressed Flower Projects

The craft of pressing flowers is a wonderfully relaxing hobby that can bring a new dimension to country walks and give an added bonus to gardening and even to growing plants in a window box. Although it is very useful to have a large garden in which to grow suitable plants for pressing, you can also press flowers and leaves picked from friends' gardens or – if you are in the middle of a city and have no other options – you will discover that your local florist may have many suitable subjects for pressing.

There are many small projects you can make from the very beginning and, with a little practice, all the projects in this book are within the capabilities of a fairly new pressed flower enthusiast. Flowers fall into different color groups and the foliage into shapes and sizes, and as you collect a variety of both, ideas for pictures should spring to mind.

Greetings card
&
Gift tag

A card made by the sender is a delightful way of marking a special occasion, and with a little extra thought you can make a gift tag to match. On the following pages are two different design ideas.

Greetings card

A design for a card can be as straightforward or as complex as you choose. Even the simplest of cards, perhaps made with just a single flower and a couple of leaves, can look most attractive and will be kept long after a purchased card would have been thrown away. Prepared blanks are available from various sources, including some stationery shops, art shops and craft suppliers. If you wish to make a matching tag, following the method overleaf, you might use one red rose backed with small raspberry leaves.

INGREDIENTS

Card blank (see page 176 for suppliers)

&

Clear film, of the type used to cover books

&

A selection of flowers and leaves

&

Latex glue

1 Lay the card on a clean surface. Using tweezers, carefully position the leaves to be used in your chosen design. This arrangement was made with a combination of blackberry leaves and Artemisia 'Lambrook Silver .

2 Add your chosen flowers, ensuring that they do not overlap leaves or stalks to any great extent. If necessary, you can trim away excess leaves and stalks that would otherwise underlie the flowers, creating ridges and lumps that might spoil the design. The flowers used for this particular design were roses and pink larkspur.

3 Using a large tapestry needle, carefully apply a little latex glue underneath each leaf and flower. When you have completed the picture and are happy with it, cut a sufficiently large rectangle of the clear film to cover the design area. Peel away the backing and then, starting from one corner, carefully lay the film over the design. The best film to use is the type that can be treated with an iron to give a better finish. Lay a piece of thin foam over the design and, with the iron on a cool setting, press firmly for about 30 seconds and then check that the result is perfect.

Gift tag

Gift tags are easy to make and offer an ideal way of introducing children to pressed flower work. The same basic method can also be used to make a bookmark, which would be a delightful and treasured gift for a much-loved grandparent. You can purchase gift card blanks or make your own from thin card. A tip if you are making your own card is to cut the card about ½in larger than the finished size and then, when the design is finished and protected with film, fold the card and trim it to size with a craft knife and metal ruler.

INGREDIENTS

Thin card or purchased gift card blank

❧

Thin crochet cotton or yarn, for a tie

❧

Clear film, of the type used to cover books

❧

A selection of flowers and leaves

❧

Latex glue

Place the card on a flat surface. Start by positioning leaves, in this case raspberry leaves, then add one or two small flowers, such as the forget-me-not sprays shown here. Finish by covering with clear film and ironing it in place, as for the card on the previous page.

Family album

This photograph frame, with its host of small family pictures, would make an excellent gift for a grandparent, although you might be tempted to keep it for yourself.

Family album

You will need to select fairly small flowers and leaves for this project, as the space available between the apertures is somewhat limited. You may be able to find a mount of this general type in stock at your local picture framer, or if not he should be able to prepare one for you (in which case you could specify a slightly more generous spacing). A fairly subtle scheme is often more successful than a very bright collection of flowers, as the latter tend to overshadow the photographs displayed.

INGREDIENTS

12in × 10in frame, with glass cut to fit and a hardboard back

❧

Mount to fit, with several apertures

❧

Family photographs

❧

A selection of small flowers and leaves

❧

Latex glue

❧

Masking tape

1 Start by assembling all the elements and considering the relationships of color and scale. Bear in mind that the space between the apertures is small and large leaves or flowers would also look out of proportion with the pictures.

2 *Choose small leaves, like the blackberry leaves used here. Lay them in position on the card, allowing them to overlap the holes slightly, if necessary.*

3 *Add some flowers to the design. This one was made with peach potentillas and 'Ballerina' roses. You might select your flowers for their sentimental associations or to blend with the decor of the album's intended setting.*

4 *Finish with some smaller flowers and delicate bits and pieces to add a dainty feel to the design – lawn daisies, small pieces of elderflower and melilot (yellow clover) were added here. Using a large needle and latex glue, secure each separate item in place. The photographs can be fixed to the back of the mount with masking tape. Cover the finished mount with the (cleaned) glass, and insert both into the frame.*

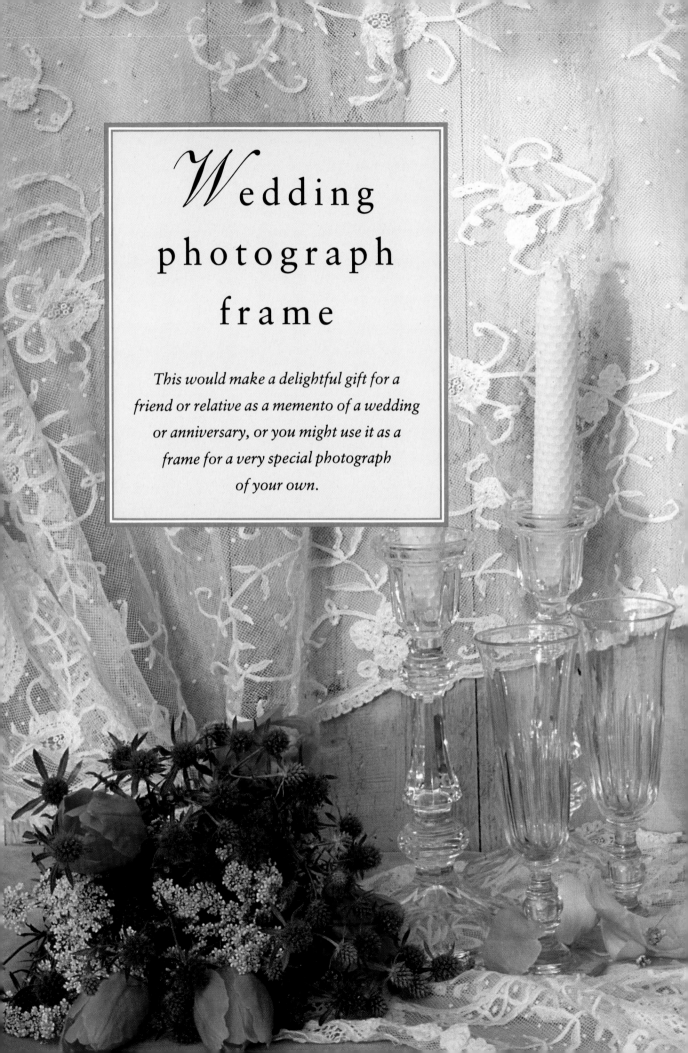

Wedding photograph frame

This would make a delightful gift for a friend or relative as a memento of a wedding or anniversary, or you might use it as a frame for a very special photograph of your own.

Wedding photograph frame

This particular design was created from flowers taken from a bride's bouquet, to add a personal and extra-romantic touch to the finished frame. Where a bride has chosen a white arrangement you could follow the Victorian example and use flower language to express the theme. Try using red rose petals for love with forget-me-nots for faithfulness, for example, as a backing for a selection of the white flowers from the bouquet. Choose a mount that has a single aperture offset, to leave plenty of space for your design.

INGREDIENTS

14in × 12in frame, with glass cut to measure and a hardboard back

❧

A mount with an offset aperture

❧

A selection of flowers, ferns and leaves

❧

Latex glue

1 Lay the mount on a clean surface and arrange some materials – in this case asparagus fern, ivy leaves and gypsophila – around the aperture, allowing them to stray a little over the edge where appropriate, to soften the photograph.

2 When the background foliage is in place, add the main flowers that will dominate the design, in this case some beautiful 'Minuet' roses. Make sure they are balanced so that the design does not look top heavy or so large as to overwhelm the photograph.

3 Finally, position the remaining elements of the design, in this case carnations and Singapore orchids, together with some additional small ivy leaves to give a little finishing touch. Using a large needle and the latex glue, glue the component parts of the arrangement firmly to the card. The photograph can then be taped in place at the back of the mount (trim it, if necessary). Give the glass a final clean to make sure there are no smears or dust, then insert the completed mount into the frame.

THE FOUR SEASONS

Spring

Creating a series of pictures to depict the seasons can offer a way of setting yourself an enjoyable challenge as you search for flowers and leaves appropriate to the period that you have in mind.

$\mathscr{S}$pring

Many spring flowers are more fragile than those pressed later in the year, so take extra care when assembling this picture. Another feature of spring flowers is that they tend to be a little translucent, so counteract this by using several, one on top of another, to create stronger color. Scale also has to be borne in mind – full-size daffodils would completely overwhelm the tiny snowdrops, but the newer miniature varieties are ideal, and can be pressed face-up or sideways.

INGREDIENTS

12in × 10in frame

୭୬

A mount with an oval aperture

୭୬

Cream silk, slightly smaller than the mount

୭୬

11in × 9in of foam, ½in thick

୭୬

Narrow masking tape

୭୬

Spring flowers and leaves

୭୬

Latex glue

୭୬

1 Stretch the silk across the back of the mount and secure with masking tape. Make sure that the silk is taut, and free from wrinkles. Place the hardboard on a clean surface, smooth side up, and lay the foam over it and the prepared mount over both.

2 Lay the leaves in position. This design used a mixture of small rose leaves and ferns.

3 Continue to build the design, adding more leaves, clustered on a focal point, together with primroses and snowdrops. The primroses can be placed one on top of another to create a greater depth of color.

4 Finally, add some more substantial flowers. This design incorporated Alchemilla mollis *leaves with small narcissi and touches of forget-me-not. Using a large needle, glue each piece in place with a little latex glue. Carefully clean the glass and place it on top of the picture. Place the frame in position and then turn the entire assembly upside down. The back can be secured with small panel pins placed at 1in intervals, or with staples (use a framer's staple gun). Seal the back with masking tape.*

THE FOUR SEASONS
Summer

Summer is the easiest time in which to find suitable subjects for pressing – indeed, you may find that you are spoiled for choice, but this is a pleasurable problem to face on an autumn evening, as you pick and choose from the summer's offerings.

$\mathcal{S}$ummer

I have used single roses for this design as they are far easier to press and seem to keep their color well. If you prefer to use hybrid tea roses, pick a newly-opened flower; strip the leaves and condition the stem by crushing it; place the rose in fairly deep water, and press just the outer petals at first, continuing to take the outer petals over two or three days as the flower opens fully. Do not press too heavily or the petals will lose their color.

INGREDIENTS

12in × 10in frame

❧

A mount with an oval aperture

❧

Cream silk, slightly smaller than the mount

❧

11in × 9in of foam, ½in thick

❧

Narrow masking tape

❧

Summer flowers and leaves

❧

Latex glue

❧

1 Prepare the mount and lay it over the hardboard and foam, as for the Spring picture (see step 1, page 24). Put spires of larkspur in the centre of the design; add two fairly large roses, and then tuck a couple of love-in-a-mist (Nigella damascena) between them.

2 Add some leaves – this example was made with maidenhair fern and chamomile leaves. Position some individual flowers of pink larkspur to mingle with all the other flowers at the centre of the design, which should now be filling out attractively while retaining the strong focus of the roses.

3 Finish with chamomile daisies and buttercups, including buds as well as flowers. Fix the flowers and leaves in position, applying a little latex glue to the back of each with a large needle. Carefully clean the glass and place it on top of the picture. Place the frame in position and then turn the entire assembly upside down. The back can be secured with small panel pins placed at 1in intervals, or with staples (use a framer's staple gun). Seal the back with masking tape.

THE FOUR SEASONS
Fall & Winter

It is not so simple to find fall or winter flowers and leaves that are suitable for pressing, but this only adds to the excitement of the chase, as you track down some new possibility.

$\mathcal{F}$all

Fall leaves are among the easiest materials to press, and even very young children can handle them as they are tough and durable. If necessary, fall leaves can even be pressed by ironing them for a couple of minutes between two sheets of blotting paper, with the iron on a medium hot setting. Artistic licence is permissible when you are creating seasonal pictures, and it is for you to decide how strictly you are going to keep to the theme.

INGREDIENTS

12in × 10in frame

❧

A mount with an oval aperture

❧

Cream silk, slightly smaller than the mount

❧

11in × 9in of foam, ½in thick

❧

Narrow masking tape

❧

Fall flowers and leaves

❧

Latex glue

❧

1 Prepare the mount and lay it over the hardboard and foam, as for the Spring picture (see step 1, page 150). Begin the design with some fall leaves – in this case, maple leaves – of a suitable golden-brown variety.

2 Add the largest flowers in the design, which will essentially be a horseshoe shape. Red and yellow roses were used here. These may not be thought of as strictly fall flowers, but some varieties have their second flowering well into the fall, so a little artistic licence is permissible.

3 Add the other small components of the design, in this case some primulas (also not truly fall blooms), some montbretia and some peach-coloured potentillas. Check the design from all angles, making sure that you have a balanced and pleasing combination. Fix the flowers and leaves in position, applying a little latex glue to the back of each with a large needle. Carefully clean the glass and place it on top of the picture.

Winter

Winter may appear to be a difficult time to collect bits and pieces for pressing, but in fact some evergreens can be pressed, and there are several flowering shrubs and plants, such as heather, that can still be picked. Make sure that your findings are dry when you put them in the press. Be experimental in your hunt for materials: lichens, mosses and skeletonised leaves are all worth pressing, and you can spray dull-coloured items with gold paint for Christmas projects.

INGREDIENTS

12in × 10in frame

A mount with an oval aperture

Cream silk, slightly smaller than the mount

11in × 9in of foam, ½in thick

Narrow masking tape

Wintery flowers and leaves

Latex glue

1 Prepare the mount and lay it over the hardboard and foam, as for the Spring picture (see step 1, page 24). Begin by establishing the leafy background; a mixture of conifer and ivy with bright red late-autumn leaves was used here.

2 Add some strong, Christmas-red roses to the centre of the design. The rose used here is a single-flowered variety called 'Robin Redbreast' – it may not be quite in season but at least the name is appropriate to the theme! Red and green bracts of euphorbia (sometimes called spurge) were also added at this stage.

3 Fill out the design with pieces of gray artemisia, heather, tiny pieces of blossom and dark red rose buds. Fix the flowers and leaves in position, applying a little latex glue to the back of each with a large needle. Carefully clean the glass and place it on top of the picture. Place the frame in position and then turn the entire assembly upside down. The back can be secured with small panel pins placed at 1in intervals, or with staples (use a framer's staple gun). Seal the back with masking tape.

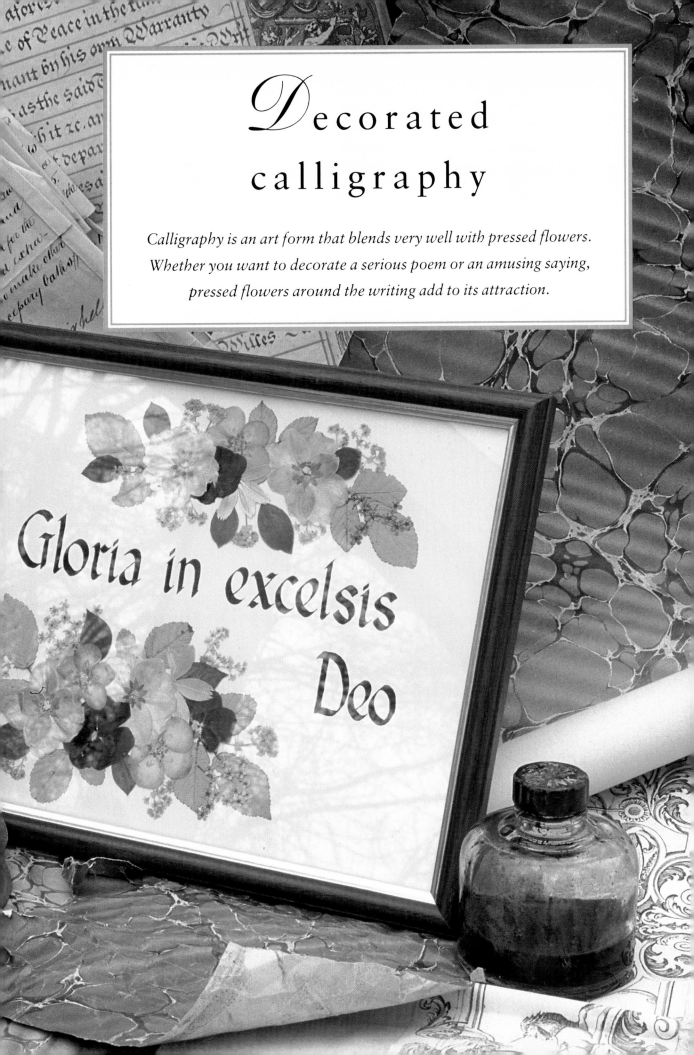

Decorated calligraphy

Calligraphy is an art form that blends very well with pressed flowers.
Whether you want to decorate a serious poem or an amusing saying,
pressed flowers around the writing add to its attraction.

Gloria in excelsis Deo

$\mathscr{A}$ baby's birth date

Whether it's your own baby or that of a friend or relative, it is a lovely idea to commemorate the new celebration day by surrounding the baby's name and birth date with pressed flowers. The result is an unusual gift that can be hung in the baby's room. If you choose, you might like to add other details, such as the baby's weight and length. This would be a charming gift to bring when you visit a new baby and mother in hospital, in which case you might like to use some of the flowers to make a matching card (see page 134).

INGREDIENTS

10in × 8in frame with glass cut to fit and a hardboard back (a photograph frame would be a suitable choice, as the background is card)

❧

Cream or pale-coloured mount, to fit the frame, with the baby's name and date of birth either in calligraphy or formed with transfers

❧

A selection of leaves and flowers

❧

Latex glue

1 Start by positioning your chosen leaves to frame the calligraphy. Silverweed (Potentilla anserina) and raspberry leaves, both of which have a lovely silvery-gray coloring, were used here.

2 Next, add dainty touches of gypsophila and heuchera, and follow these with the large flowers, in this case a hedging variety of rose with semi-double flowers.

3 To finish, add some more flowers – pink larkspur and hydrangea florets, the latter with potentilla centres forming the middles. When you are happy with the design, secure each item with latex glue, applying it with a large needle. Cover the finished picture with clean glass and then fix it in the frame.

Gloria in excelsis

If you are not able to produce beautiful calligraphy – and it is an art form that requires practice – then try using a clear, copperplate style or just your ordinary handwriting. It is possible to buy special italic-style felt-tips from art shops, or you might find it easier to use transfers. Practise the spacing on scrap paper before using the cream card. You may find it helpful to make a sample on tracing paper and lay this over the card to check the effect.

INGREDIENTS

10in × 8in frame with glass cut to fit and a hardboard back (a photograph frame would be a suitable choice, as the background is card)

❧

Cream or pale-coloured mount, to fit the frame, with the chosen piece of calligraphy

❧

A selection of leaves and flowers

❧

Latex glue

1 Write your chosen text and then place some leaves around the writing. Blackberry leaves were used here, positioned upside down to show their beautiful gray undersides.

166

2 Having established the frame of the design with the larger leaves, begin to fill it out with some smaller ones. In this particular example, some small fall leaves and sprays of Alchemilla mollis were used.

3 Finish by positioning the larger flowers in the design. Here, cream Anemone japonica *were combined with some dark maroon pansies and a peach potentilla. The centres of the anemones are in fact spare potentilla middles. (When pressing flowers with fairly hard centres, it is easier to remove the centres and either press them separately or discard them and use a false centre, such as a centre from a potentilla or daisy, or a cow parsley floret.) When you are happy with the design, secure each item with glue, with a large needle. Cover the picture with clean glass and then fix it in the frame.*

Terracotta bowl & Garden posy

Pressed flower pictures can take many forms, and fresh arrangements can inspire a range of ideas. Two of these are shown here, and hopefully they may lead you to develop your own designs.

Terracotta bowl

Containers can be made from plant material, thin cardboard or fabric; this terracotta bowl is made from thin mount cardboard and looks very effective. Any colour can be used to make a vase of your choice; alternatively, you might use cotton fabric with a paisley or floral print to make a decorated vase. Beech leaves can give the effect of wood, while glass effects can be created with honesty seed pods.

INGREDIENTS

10in × 8in frame, and mount to fit, with large oval aperture

❧

Cream or white silk, slightly smaller than the mount, and 9in × 7in of foam, ½in thick

❧

4in × 6in of thin terracotta-colored cardboard

❧

Selection of leaves and flowers

❧

Narrow masking tape

❧

Latex glue

1 Prepare the mount and lay it over the hardboard and foam, as for the Spring picture (see step 1, page 24). Cut out a bowl shape from the terracotta mount card, drawing the shape on the back in pencil and then cutting it out with a craft knife.

2 Place the bowl on the mounted silk, and start positioning the leaves, in this case wild geranium and raspberry. A small spray lying by the base of the bowl adds an extra touch of interest and helps to balance the picture.

3 Next, position the largest flowers. Anemone japonica have been used face-down here, as the underside of the petals has a pretty shimmer. With the anemones in place, some other small items – wormwood flowers and rue leaves – could be added.

4 Fill out the design with 'Ballerina' roses and potentillas ('Miss Willmot'), and then some more leaves. The spray at the bottom may lie to the right or left – the choice is yours. Fix the flowers and leaves in position, applying a little latex glue to the back of each with a large needle. Carefully clean the glass and place it on top of the picture. Place the frame in position and then turn the entire assembly upside down. The back can be secured with small panel pins placed at 1in intervals, or with staples (use a framer's staple gun). Seal the back with masking tape.

Garden posy

This design features an informal posy, made with flowers that are easily grown in a small garden. A picture of a bridal bouquet could also be made in this style, and you might incorporate ribbons from the original bouquet, or perhaps a scrap of lace from the bride's dress. In a similar vein, you might preserve some flowers from a Mother's Day bouquet to make a picture of this type. To do this, you would have to remove some of the flowers for pressing while they were still at their peak, but the sacrifice would be worth making for a year-round reminder of a happy occasion.

INGREDIENTS

8in × 6in frame, with glass to fit and a hardboard back

❧

Mount to fit, with a large oval aperture

❧

White or cream silk, slightly smaller than the mount, and 7in × 5in of foam, ½in thick

❧

Garden flowers and leaves, with some long stalks

❧

Narrow masking tape

❧

Latex glue

❧

1 Prepare the mount and lay it over the hardboard and foam, as for the Spring picture (see step 1, page 24). Place the stalks in position and make a circle of leaves (in this case, raspberry and mugwort).

2 Add to the posy hydrangea florets, roses and larkspur, tucking the flowers so that they are not all piled on top of each other. Finish with smaller elements, such as forget-me-nots and small cream potentillas. Complete the picture as for the bowl (step 4, page 45).

Pressing flowers

You need only a minimum amount of equipment to press flowers successfully. The first item is a flower press. Although you can use old books, there are many small flowers and leaves that are best treated in a traditional press. Since presses are very simple to make and cheap to buy it is preferable to use one to start with.

If you do not wish to use a traditional flower press, telephone books, which have absorbent pages, offer a practical alternative. You will need to put further books or other weights on top of the book in order to give some pressure.

Most pressed flower pictures can be made with a standard craft glue, which is a latex adhesive. This rubs off if you spill some on the card on which you are laying your flowers, but it may leave a mark. It holds the flowers well, however, and does not produce any brown marks on the pressed materials, or at least not for some time.

PRESSING

If your press is a purchased model, begin by discarding the corrugated cardboard inside the press – the cardboard tends to leave unsightly lines across the pressed flowers. Start with a layer of newspaper, then cover this with a sheet of blotting paper. Lay the flowers on the blotting paper, making sure that none of them overlap and all are well within the edges of the blotting paper. Cover the flowers with another layer of blotting paper and then more newspaper. The next layer starts with another sheet of blotting paper, and you can continue until you have ten layers of flowers in the press. Cover this last layer with blotting paper and then newspaper, and screw the press down as firmly as possible.

Label your press clearly, listing the contents and the date on which they went into the press. It is also useful to add where you picked the flowers. Otherwise you may find, when you open the press and are delighted with its contents, that you have no idea where the flowers came from.

Put the labelled press in a warm place – such as a warm closet – where the temperature will remain fairly constant. Leave it for between six and eight weeks, by which time the flowers will be dried and pressed. Resist the temptation to open the press too early in order to look and see how things are progressing; pressed flowers are very delicate while they are drying, and you may damage them.

If you are using a telephone book instead of a press, place the flowers or leaves between sheets of blotting paper. Several books with blotting paper folders inside can be piled up. It is still, of course, important to label them just as you would label a press.

STORAGE AND PROTECTION

Once the flowers are ready, you can remove them from the press and keep them in clear-fronted paper bags. Never store pressed flowers in polythene bags as they will sweat and go mouldy.

Pressed flower pictures should always be hung out of the light – bright light will cause the color in the flowers and leaves to fade. However, a picture made with pressed materials that have been chosen for their good quality and their color retention can be hung in a shady place and will continue to look attractive for many years. There are pictures that are six years old in my house, and they still look as good as new, but I do live in a very old cottage, with small windows that restrict the amount of light to which the pictures are subjected.

Choosing Your Materials

Many flowers and leaves are suitable for pressing, but those that are naturally flatter are much easier to press than multi-petalled varieties, such as carnations or tea roses. If you want to press one of the latter, then it must be taken to pieces petal by petal, pressed, and then reassembled when used in a picture.

Some flowers keep their color dramatically better than others, and this can be discovered by trial and error from among the flowers available to each individual. As a rough guideline, pale pinks and peach tones can be very difficult to retain, whereas oranges and fall shades tend to be strong and last for a long time. A good way to test the colorfast properties of a plant is to press a selection of flowers taken from it; place these under glass on a sunny windowsill for a couple of weeks, and see what happens. Keep notes, and press more of those materials that keep their color well, avoiding anything that fades too quickly.

Blue delphiniums and all the larkspur family make excellent subjects for pressing, as do most gray and silvery leaves. Ignore succulents, as these contain too much water, and avoid flowers that have particularly thick centres, such as large daisies or chrysanthemums.

Very little equipment is required, but a flower press is a useful investment.